Ministerial Ethics & Etiquette

Ministerial Ethics & Etiquette

REVISED EDITION

NOLAN B. HARMON

NASHVILLE
•
ABINGDON

MINISTERIAL ETHICS AND ETIQUETTE

ISBN 0-687-27033-2
Library of Congress Catalog Card Number: 50-8100

MANUFACTURED BY THE PARTHENON PRESS AT
NASHVILLE, TENNESSEE, UNITED STATES OF AMERICA

To
the Memory of

MY MOTHER

Juliet Howe Harmon

WHO TAUGHT ME
WAYS OF GENTLENESS
AS WELL AS OF
CHRISTIAN LIVING

CONTENTS

INTRODUCTION

It goes without saying that the minister is a Christian, and it goes with this saying that he is a gentleman. This is the base line of the code assembled in the following pages. It is accepted as an axiom that every minister is a Christian gentleman.

It has long been my belief that the true Christian will always know how to conduct himself everywhere. That does not mean that the moment a man or minister is consecrated to God he will automatically know "which fork to use first," or understand all the vagaries of social protocol. The fashion of this world changeth and so do the pretty—and petty—little customs that prevail among ladies and gentlemen. But beneath the whole range of matters discussed in the "Blue Book"—knives and forks, soup and fish, the cutting of cabbages and the treatment of kings—there are a few deep principles; and these principles, the postulates upon which gentlemen act, are not far from a Christian ethic. A gentleman may not be a Christian, but a Christian must always be a gentleman. If urbane men of the world can achieve a high plane of courtesy and honor, surely the men of God can do no less. Old, naïve, unsophisticated ministers, ignorant of all the usages of polite society but saturated with the grace of God through years of service, sometimes show in face and bearing a graceful tenderness and an air of Christian courtliness that the halls of Versailles might well have envied. *Unselfishness*, or a pretense to it, underlies the whole code of proper conduct in the "Blue Book," but with the Christian it cannot be pretense. Taking thought for others is the essence of ministerial ethics and etiquette.

Until comparatively recent years no serious attempt has been made to draw up anything like a code of ministerial ethics. In the very nature of things nothing like a binding code of ethical conduct can be drawn, for it would be impossible to get general agreement among ministers on many points having to do with manners and morals. Many churches and sects today cannot agree on some of the greater moral issues. How then can they be expected to agree upon minor matters having to do with moot points of ethical conduct or, in some instances, mere etiquette? Furthermore, even if there were agreement on these matters, there is not and cannot be any interdenominational court or tribunal to enforce upon any minister a system governing his morals or his conduct. He is a law unto himself. If his fathers went to war to prevent some church or king from telling them how they should kneel or stand or sit at Communion, he is not going to let anyone today tell him how to make a pastoral call, or what church publicity he may properly use. The whole system of Protestantism is wound up with the individual's rights in this matter.

Also it should be noted that the various denominations have their special regulations governing their own ministers on matters of ethical conduct, and other questions they leave to the obligation of every minister to keep the moral law and live as a Christian. The Protestant Episcopal Church for instance has its canon law, The Methodist Church its *Discipline*, the Presbyterian Church, U.S.A., its *Book of Church Order*, and other Christian groups their customs and long-time practices. To these the men of the respective churches look for guidance and authority on many questions of ethical procedure.

It should be mentioned also that the minister himself is supposed to be an arbiter in the field of morals and ethics; and, since he is personally regarded as a judge and divider in such matters, he is trusted to regulate his own conduct properly. As soon expect—it might be argued—a medical association to draw up health rules for physicians or to issue a book on what medicine is good for a doctor, as to expect ministers to tell each other what courses of moral and ethical conduct are proper.

Last but not least it must be admitted that many of the matters involved are not of great moment. They have to do with jots and tittles and scarcely ever touch the inflexible bulwarks and buttresses of the moral law. When a matter does go over into a question of morals, then the minister's conscience, not to say his church, speaks up.

Nevertheless in spite of all this there has gradually evolved through the years a strong consciousness of ministerial brotherhood, and this brotherhood has a definite feeling that it ought to be able to say something about the conduct of its own members. Perhaps this growing ministerial solidarity has its dangers. Henry Ward Beecher in his day thought so and decried the idea that the ministry should stick together as a unit. However, it is undeniable that an intangible but powerful professional consciousness has come to be felt among ministers today. As denominational walls have gone down, ministers of all groups and communions have felt themselves to be closer kin, true brothers one to another. The result has been that while the sanctions and findings of ministerial custom cannot be considered as binding upon any man, they can be considered as advisory and suggestive to a high degree. While no code of ministerial ethics could ever be enforced by positive sanctions, nor should it be, the opinions and approved practices of one's ministerial compeers must necessarily be regarded with great respect. Like international law which gets its sanction from world opinion, ministerial ethical judgments must get theirs, not from an "interdenominational police force," but from the common sense of the ministry itself.

It has been clear for some time that there is a continuing interest in and need for an up-to-date comprehensive outline of ministerial practices and professional ethical judgments. The various codes of ministerial ethics which have appeared have long testified to this need. This book itself, originally published over a score of years ago, has served to focus attention on the fact that ministers do feel the need for a systematic treatment of the many personal and ethical problems connected with their life work. It has been revised in answer to a demand that some of its statements and findings be brought up to date, that newer techniques and present-day methods of managing certain situations which were not prominent a generation ago be properly dealt with, and that more detailed treatment be accorded certain situations in which a minister's professional service should be at its best.

In revising this book I have continued to depend on the series of formal ministerial codes drawn up a score of years ago by various ecclesiastical groups: the *Congregational Code*, adopted by the New Haven, Connecticut, Association of Congregational Ministers and found on pages 25-27 of *Church Administration*, by William H. Leach; the *Methodist Code*, said to have been adopted by a conference of Methodist ministers at Rockwood, Illinois, in 1926, and printed in the *Christian Century*, December 16, 1926; the *Presbyterian Code*, said to have been adopted by the New York Presbytery, and printed in an article by Leach in the *Methodist Quarterly Review*, July, 1927; and the *Unitarian Code*, adopted by the Unitarian Ministerial Union and found in *Church Management*, August, 1926. These codes are now supplemented by the *Disciples Code*, published in 1945 by the Committee on Effective Ministry of the Home and State

Missions Planning Council of Disciples of Christ and found in *Called—In Honor*, by Charles B. Tupper (published by Bethany Press).

These codes will be found printed in their entirety in the appendix to this volume. Careful inquiry has been made to discover what, if any, changes have been made through the years. No alterations have been found, and presumably the codes remain in force in their respective situations just as they were when adopted. Their findings are such as to elicit widespread approval, and in no instance has a single item of any one of them been spoken against. These codes are therefore held foremost as a frame of reference and are cited at all points throughout this book.

But in order to obtain more direct and empirical knowledge, and to obtain from ministers themselves a common mind regarding many points of professional procedure, eighty-six carefully selected clergymen from over the nation have been relied upon as mentors and advisors in the revision of this book. Each of these ministers represents a commanding pulpit, and many of them are nationally known. They are all pastors with the possible exception of two or three, and those few are known to have had long pastoral experience. They are all men who are looked upon with respect as outstanding pastors, not only by their own denominational family, but by the entire populace in the region where each resides. Every part of the country is represented and all major denominations; although the number called upon for this service was comparatively small, the quality of the men replying and the influence and the leadership which each exercises guarantee reliable and authoritative answers.

Each of these mentors was given a comprehensive series of questions dealing with attitudes and situations which are puzzling to the ordinary minister. His judgment, advice, or practice was asked in each instance, and in addition comment was invited up-on all that seemed germane.

The response of those men was generous, and in many in-stances terse comment or advice gave additional insight and help. Their replies have been carefully collated and the result made known at the appropriate place in the following pages. Where there is a division of opinions or where practices differ, this too is noted.

In addition to the codes cited and the ministerial authorities relied on, I have continued to refer to such books and articles as may be helpful, attempting to catch together in this book all suggestions, thoughts, and directions which might be obtained from the writings and expressed judgments of ministers which would aid in clarifying the points at issue.

In arranging the material I have endeavored to give the most space to the most debatable questions, and to make the work comprehensive while omitting the trite and dismissing with a bare mention the obvious. The general Christian consciousness has been drawn on for many sanctions where no definite author-ity could be cited. It was of course impossible to cover all re-lationships, just as it is impossible to classify all those relation-ships correctly by chapter and division, since this is an arbitrary matter. Above all I wish to make clear that in no way do I set myself up as an *arbiter elegantiarum*, but simply as one who is glad to assemble the thought and judgment of my fellow minis-ters and weld it together in the hope that the result as set forth may be helpful to all.

A word may be said here about combining ministerial etiquette with ministerial ethics. Some who are impressed by the ethical demands of their profession are not always impressed by the need for the proper amenities of social procedure. They might, however, consider what was said by a wise old bishop once in addressing a group of his younger clergy on the importance "of little ways of gentleness that endear preachers to people":

Although these things may not come up to the dignity of minor morals, I submit to you that this is one of the cases where it does well to tithe mint and anise and cumin. If by attention to these things we can make ourselves more useful, it is well worth while to attend to them. Of course a minister does not forfeit his soul because he does not know how to enter and leave a parlor; he has not committed a mortal sin because he cannot make a graceful bow; he has not offended against the Holy Ghost because he always wears a somber countenance instead of a smiling face. But if these things have so much to do with our success as ministers of Christ, I submit to you if our text (Rom. 16:1-15) teaches no other lesson but that of courtesy, it is well worth our learning.

It was said of a beloved English cleric that "when he went up to the high altar, he made the garments of God honorable." The Christian minister today, whether conducting some impressive rite of his church, or preaching the Word, or ministering to the poor, or perhaps helping his wife in some menial task about the home, has the opportunity at all times to make honorable the calling in which God has placed him.

CHAPTER I

The Christian Ministry

By common consent the Christian ministry is esteemed the noblest of the professions. Some may object to this classification, and some may wish it qualified by affirming that by the Christian ministry is meant a real ministry and not a counterfeit one. General consent, however, does give to the ministry primacy among the noble callings. If this much be accorded by persons other than the minister, he himself certainly ought to hold his profession in as high regard as does the world. Many ministers believe it to be higher in kind as well as degree, but they never press this upon others. They take the recognition of their "high calling," not as a mark of personal honor to themselves, but as an honor to that One who first called them. Like the Apostle, the best minister strives to apprehend that for which he was himself apprehended.

From this acknowledged truth that the ministry is the highest form of professional service spring several principles that form the axioms on which any consideration of the minister's conduct must be based:

1. *The minister must keep the nobility of his calling uppermost in his own mind.* Should he fail to do this, he had better take up some other form of work. If for any cause he begins to look down upon his profession, or to feel that for him its glory has departed, he is lost. The temptation may come to him,

for instance, to measure the ministry by some of the standards which apply to the work of other professions—by temporal influence, by cultural values, by that ubiquitous and omnipresent measure of all things in our day and time, money. But should he attempt to use any of these things as a measure for his work, failure will come to him. The Christian ministry can no more be measured by these values than time can be measured by the mile or space by the pound. The professional standards of the ministry belong to another category, a spiritual one, nevertheless a very real one. Any effort to force a comparison with other professions will fail. The Christian minister must know this. He who deprecates his calling in his own mind or who doubts its value for him is in a bad way. Let the story of Sir Lancelot and the lions be recalled. When, as Tennyson gives it to us, the beasts uprose and each grasped the knight by a shoulder, a voice came saying:

> Doubt not, go forward; if thou doubt, the beasts
> Will tear thee piecemeal.

So the man who doubts in his own mind the mission and work of his own calling is in a fair way to be torn piecemeal between the twin lions of hopelessness and despair. He who doubts not, but goes forward believing, will find the world believing with him.[1]

2. *The minister must hold high in outward acts the established reputation of the Christian ministry.* There is a popular esteem in which the ministry is held, a popular regard, estimation, and measure, not the making of one generation but of all generations. It is entirely possible for some one minister to lower or injure

[1] "The minister should never speak disparagingly of his church or his profession." (*Unitarian Code*, I, 6.)

this popular estimation. When this happens, a man's excuse may be that prevalent conceptions as to ministerial rights and privileges are wrong, and therefore he is engaged in an attempt to set them right. Or he may say that new occasions teach new duties, etc. But every minister should weigh very carefully his own thought and intent against the practice of the ages. Just as no reputable lawyer ever breaks the traditions of his ancient and honorable calling, just as no physician departs from but holds in the highest respect his own professional ethics and methods, so the ministry should preserve and guard those traits which by a common consent belong to the highest type of ministerial service.

It would be impossible to list all the various ways in which ministers may lower the popular estimation in which their profession is held, but that it can be lowered all know. Perhaps ministers should have some such custom as prevails among army officers. There is a charge for which military and naval officers are sometimes court-martialed known as "conduct unbecoming an officer and a gentleman." What this conduct is cannot be specified beforehand—each case is brought to trial upon its own merits. Sometimes it is for one thing, sometimes for another, occasionally even for unprecedented breaches in official bearing. On all such occasions the officers themselves act as judges of this vague, intangible, but all-embracing law. Cannot the same standard be applied to the conduct of ministers?—for there are acts which are unbecoming a minister as well as those unbecoming a gentleman.

For instance in the name of "pulpit freedom" or of "necessary showmanship" some ministers have frankly become publicity seekers. The minister who thus breaks a thousand years of pulpit tradition (and this can be done in a thousand ways) may receive "two sticks" notice in all the papers and be flattered as one "free from ancient shackles"; but it is the part of wisdom to await the final fruits of this man's life and acts. This is not to plead for a narrow-grooved ministry, nor for conformity to traditionalism as such, but one may well be suspicious of the brother who is so anxious to show himself "free" that he wears the clothes of a clown in order that he may not be taken for a "gentleman of the cloth," or who turns his pulpit into a vaudeville stage to show that no bondage of pulpit formality is binding on him. Such men more often than not give the impression that they are lovers of publicity more than lovers of God, more anxious to proclaim themselves than their Lord. Buffoonery has no place in the pulpit of God, nor may a minister lend himself to stunt marriages, mock funerals, or any other act which marks down his holy calling. Care should be taken by each minister that his public and private conduct be not unbecoming to the best traditions of his profession.

The story is told that a minister once decided that he would go upon the grounds of a certain college in Pennsylvania—a college whose charter, as is well known, prohibits any minister of the gospel from setting foot upon its grounds. The minister in question disguised himself and achieved his object; he got in. But here is the point: he had to sail under false colors to do it, and ministers everywhere, universally, refuse to forswear their calling for a moment. On the contrary they are proud of their profession, nor is there any special regret among them because they are forbidden to visit the college in question. No gentleman ever cares to go where not wanted.

Conduct unbecoming a gentleman is always conduct unbecoming a minister, but conduct sometimes not unbecoming in other gentlemen may be unbecoming in the minister. Henry Wilder Foote, in his *The Minister and His Parish*, observed that the community expects a closer adherence to moral standards on the part of the minister than from the ordinary man; that there are "courses of conduct which, while all right for others, are unbecoming in him." This is quite true. A different ethical sense governs the minister from that which the ordinary gentleman recognizes. A minister may rebel, and with good logic too, at the implications of this statement. He may affirm that he has a perfect right to do what any other Christian has the right to do—and theoretically he has. *Practically*, however, he is going to find, as Lloyd C. Douglas expressed it, that the people will make a priest out of him whether he likes it or not. He will discover that he is bound not only by the law of the gentleman, but by something more, which may be called by various names. However, the scriptural term *expediency* probably best describes this principle which, while not always binding upon others, must always be considered by the minister. Paul expressed this apropos of his own Christian right: "All things are lawful unto me, but all things are not expedient." (I Cor. 6:12.) We need not push into the Apostle's deeper meaning here, but the successful pastor is going to learn that while certain customs, habits, manners, and viewpoints of his own may be logical, sane, and correct, it will not always be expedient for him to thrust them forward as such. Not that principles must be toned down, or that expediency itself may not sometimes be made an excuse for moral cowardice and compromise; but it is true that things which for the man may be lawful, may for the minister not be expedient.

For instance, a certain minister was a great smoker of tobacco. After service one Sunday evening he walked home with one of his leading men. As the pair approached the house the layman turned to his pastor and said: "Brother N——, if you will not be offended at my request, I am going to ask that you do not let my boys see you smoking. They admire you very much and I

21

do not wish them to be influenced by your example and, while they are young, learn the use of tobacco." Now the pastor might have entered upon a strong argument in defense of his right to smoke, and might perhaps have proved his case. He might have gone into a dissertation upon tobacco as something lawful if lawfully used. He might even have made a matter of principle of it, and said that he felt it right to stand fast in the liberty in which he had been made free, and that he could not afford to give away his Christian liberty and that of others by yielding in this regard. As a matter of fact he said nothing, but did as he was asked. He threw away his cigar and "quit" from then on. He said later that if he had any habit which prevented him from exerting the best sort of influence over the young men of his church, that habit was wrong—and his statement was right.

So with many points of conduct. It is perfectly lawful for a minister to associate himself with a social group which has nothing in common with his own flock, but the time may come when he will find that it was not expedient. It is perhaps lawful for the minister to tell the loudest and best of all his jokes at the Sunday dinner table when he is "company" somewhere; but when that man again stands in his pulpit and reads the "watch and be sober" phrases which were written, not at a Roman banquet, but in the lurid glow of fiery persecution throwing its shadows against an eternal background, he is going to find that it was not quite expedient.

In the attempt to be good mixers some ministers have used expressions and even told off-color stories which they hoped would prove them to be "like other men." They little realize what they lose by this even in the estimation of those whom they would impress. Dr. Foote had it right—whether we like it or not, the people demand a higher standard from the minister than from the ordinary man.

3. *The minister must never forget that he is one who serves—* and that he must be on guard against a temptation which his very profession presents to him. He occupies a position in the local church and congregation which puts him upon a pedestal in the minds of the people. Everything serves to dramatize the centrality of his place as pastor, preacher, and executive; and long continued and unchallenged leadership often intensifies this pre-eminence. His opinions in the official church meetings are quite often listened to by able businessmen as though an oracle were pronouncing, and his least wish is sometimes regarded as something divinely ordered. It is no wonder that men in the ministry, if they are not careful, will tend to think more highly of themselves than they ought to think (and there have been instances where successful ministers delivered their personal opinions and judgments with an assurance of complete infallibility). Ministers' wives often perceive this magisterial attitude on the part of their husbands before the man himself is aware of it. Every minister ought, of course, to lead; but his leadership should be tempered with a deep-seated awareness of his own fallibility, and he should never forget what manner of man he is. A sense of humor, as well as a common-sense wife and a plain-spoken friend or two in the church, will act as a saving remedy here, and while a man should take his work seriously he should never take himself too much so. Every minister should be on guard against "pre-eminence setting in."

4. *The minister must never for reasons of personal safety desert his parish and people when some great, universal danger impends,* such as a hostile invasion, a virulent epidemic, or natural disaster. Happily this situation seldom arises—has arisen only a few times in our own land—but the unanimous voice of the ministers of all the ages has declared that the pastor may not leave his people and fly to safety when the people themselves

23

are in some epochal danger. His own family he may send to safety or protect when he can; indeed in visiting those with contagious diseases he must be extraordinarily careful to protect his home; but for himself there must be faithfulness unto death. It is in times of natural disaster, floods, epidemics, earthquakes, bloodshed, that the pastor may prove a tower of strength to his flock. If the captain of the ship is the last man to step into the lifeboat; if the engineer, grimy with soot, makes it his first consideration to save the train, let what will happen to the locomotive, surely ministers of Christ can stay at their posts during times that try their people's souls, giving comfort and help and rescue.

This question was discussed at great length in Possidius' *Life of Saint Augustine*. It seems that the barbarians were laying waste all North Africa and were advancing to besiege Hippo. The ministers with others were deserting the churches and fleeing before them. Augustine, Bishop of Hippo, was asked by many priests what course they should pursue. They were not cowards, but doubted the wisdom of remaining and giving their lives for a problematical good. Many persons had fled, though some refused to leave. Augustine, the great church father, sat down and wrote a letter about it. It is solid Latin (and Augustine could write some of the most involved as well as some of the clearest Latin ever composed by mortal man), but out of the uncouth language of a bygone age a mighty spirit and great man makes himself entirely clear. It is not right, said Augustine, to close the churches; it is not right for the shepherd to flee when the flock is to be left—the priest of God must stay at his post. Today the universal voice of the Christian ministry says he was right.

One of the distinguished authorities relied upon by this book insists that the rule against a pastor deserting his people in time of peril or emergency applies also to a minister leaving a local church in what may be for it a time of crisis. When some large building enterprise or heavy financial plan has been undertaken (especially at the behest of the pastor), or when a fire or other disaster has struck heavily at a congregation's resources, no pastor should at such a time pack up and take a pulpit elsewhere. That there is validity in this assertion is, of course, granted; but it would be difficult to maintain that no pastor should ever leave a church, or accept a call to another pulpit, as long as the church he is then serving is in difficulties. Most churches have problems of various sorts arising continually, and the church without difficulties has yet to be discovered. Circumstances here as elsewhere would seem to govern in this matter—the degree of involvement or the progress made in some pending plan, as well as the pastor's responsibility for leading the church into it. No minister worthy of the name, after persuading his parishioners to undertake some heavy financial burden or leading them to commit themselves to some momentous plan, would forthwith feel free to leave these parishioners immediately upon receiving a call to greener—and less onerous—pastures. Such moves have been made, of course, and may be made again, in the working out of the ministerial system. But many a minister has spoiled his record in a place by his manner of leaving it; and the minister who must follow such a person will have a much heavier task, thanks (or no thanks) to the predecessor.

5. *The minister must utilize his time properly.* Like other professions, the ministry is not a matter of eight working hours with pay-and-a-half for overtime, but of life service. The minister therefore gives himself completely to his profession. Of course this does not preclude days off, vacation periods, etc., which belong to all professional men; but the minister feels that his profession demands his all. To engage for a certain part of his time

in other remunerative work would, he believes, break into the usefulness of his calling. He would consider it a lowering of the legal profession should he learn that a certain lawyer acted as night watchman during part of his time, or a letting down of the medical profession if he found that a physician in off hours acted as bookkeeper for a manufacturing concern. Not that these other occupations are not eminently worthy and fully as estimable as are the professions mentioned above if engaged in honorably, as they should be—but professional men universally hold that their profession demands their all.[2]

The ministry is often tempted to depart from this professional rule. Salaries are low and in some places it becomes almost a necessity for the minister to help supplement his salary by engaging in other occupations. This is bad—bad for the man, bad for the calling, and bad for the people. Where there is any other choice this should not be done. However, the hard but unanswerable fact is that sometimes it must be done. But consequences take no thought of excuses. The preacher who is compelled to buy and sell on the side, or to teach school for a remuneration, will find that his ministerial standing suffers, no matter how good may be the reasons which impel him to divide his work. The minister will do well to avoid any work outside his own professional labor. In case he must engage in other remunerative work, however, he should have a clear understanding about this matter with the officials of his local church.[3]

[2] "As a minister controls his own time, he should make it a point of honor to give full service to his parish." (*Congregational Code*, I, 1. The *Methodist* and *Presbyterian Codes* similar.)

"I will dedicate my time and energy to my Christian ministry and will maintain strict standards of discipline." (*Disciples Code*, II.)

[3] "It is unethical for the minister to engage in other lines of remunerative work without the knowledge and consent of the Church or its official board." (*Congregational Code*, II, 3.)

6. *The minister must never measure his work by the salary involved.* It is the just pride of all the professions that they place service above profit, but no matter what may be the case with others, this rule may never be forgotten nor deviated from by the ministry. The whole matter of ministerial remuneration could be discussed at great length, and local and national economics, personal abilities, and special regional and ecclesiastical customs and regulations are all involved. However, after all has been written or said the rule cited above will stand unshaken. The laborer is worthy of his hire and must have it; but with the Christian ministry it is the work and not the wages which must be supreme.[4]

As a corollary it should be said that just as the minister should not measure his own services in terms of money, neither should he so measure that of any brother minister. The "grading" of ministers by the size of their respective salaries is a degrading of the whole profession.

Using the ministerial or priestly position to get financial gain for one's self has long been known as *simony*. Technically, *simony* is "traffic in that which is sacred; specif., the buying and selling of ecclesiastical preferment." This of course has always been despised by the true men of the ministry. However, the man who measures every bit of professional service by its monetary equivalent, or who thinks in terms of money, is not far removed from the one who would sell spiritual gifts for silver or gold.

There is a subtle form of ministerial danger in which some have become involved, though not as much in recent years as

[4] "As a professional man the minister should make his service primary and the remuneration secondary. His efficiency, however, demands that he receive a salary adequate to the work he is expected to do and commensurate with the scale of living in that parish which he serves." (*Congregational Code*, II, 2. The *Methodist Code* is practically identical.)

earlier in the century. This is the use of the pastoral position or ministerial standing as a means of influencing the financial transactions of others, notably one's church members. Sometimes the minister himself has gone into financial dealings for private gain. Some have bought and sold stock in certain concerns or have promoted and sold stock among their own members. In some cases it is in real estate that these transactions take place, and ministers, after becoming involved themselves, draw their people in. Such proceedings hardly ever result in financial profit and never result in spiritual gain. Sometimes the loss is both financial and spiritual and church and ministry both suffer. This temptation is usually brought to the minister by some interested person—the popular pastor is often sought out and invited to "get in" a promising transaction. He is perhaps allowed a liberal premium or given a large block of the first shares of the new company. His influence is recognized and his name will lend sanctity, though not always salvation, to the speculation. But let the minister beware. If trustful people under the care of their pastor follow him and get hurt in a financial undertaking, that pastor will have to face a terrible judgment at the bar of his own conscience. The business of the minister is to lead people along spiritual lines, not to aid them or even himself in making money. Let the minister shun all such invitations.[5]

Years ago the distinguished Dr. Newell Dwight Hillis of Brooklyn made the mistake of engaging in certain timber speculations which turned out badly for him and for some of his friends. Dr. Hillis confessed the whole matter to his congregation publicly and asked forbearance. This story is told here not

[5] "The minister should always place service above profit, avoiding the suspicion of an inordinate love of money, and never measuring his work by his salary." (*Unitarian Code*, I, 1.)

to reflect upon this good and great minister but to recall the magnificent statement he made at that time:

> For years I have had a growing conviction that a minister has no right to make money, and does his best work without it. . . . At best the longest life is short, all too short for the noblest of tasks, that of the Christian minister. Great is the influence of the law and medicine; wonderful is the task of the jurist and statesman; marvelous the power of the press; great also the opportunity of the merchant and manufacturer who feed and clothe the people; but nothing can be higher than the call to shepherd Christ's poor and weak, and happy the minister who has never interpreted his ministry in terms of intellect alone, or has never secularized his sacred calling, and who at the end of his life is able to say: Behold these are the sheep thou gavest me, and not one of them is lost.[6]

These words should be taken to heart by every minister. Let all temptation to make money "on the side" be eschewed. The minister's meat is to do the Father's will. Let him remember that in the division of land to the twelve tribes, as narrated in the Old Testament, the Levites got no share of land for a possession. "The Lord" was to be their inheritance. "The Lord spake unto Aaron, Thou shalt have no inheritance in their land. . . . *I* am thy part and thine inheritance among the children of Israel." (Num. 18:20.)

7. *The minister must guard the use of his name.* He should not give the sanction of his endorsement to those causes or movements of which he cannot be sure. Men and women of prominence, ministers among them, have often had cause to regret the fact that they permitted their names to be used on the letterhead of this, that, or the other supposedly charitable or benevo-

---

[6] *Literary Digest,* November 23, 1915.

lent organization. Quite often the purpose and methods of these hastily organized associations are commendable, but other things, such as unsavory agents or questionable advertising methods, sometimes make the minister or public man wish he had never heard of the organization which he has so openly—and hastily— endorsed. People of prominence are usually drawn into giving their names for use in such work by being assured that the purpose is beneficent, and that the name is all that they need give; no details of the work will fall on them. That is true; the name is all that is wanted—but how valuable that is! The minister should make it a rule never to give his name to any organization or movement to which he cannot at the same time give himself and, within limits, his attention. This will force him to know what he is getting into, and will give him a chance to have an actual voice in the project. Needless to say, good taste forbids public, paid testimonials, especially by ministers, in behalf of some commercial product.[7]

After the Civil War ended General Robert E. Lee was of course penniless, but his fame had gone far and wide. The story goes that he was sought by a certain powerful financial concern which was organizing an insurance company and wished to have *his name* as the president of the concern. It was explained that the ex-commander would have no actual duties at all, although a princely salary would be given him; that what the company really wanted was his name. General Lee heard the men through and then said simply, "Gentlemen, I have nothing left but my name, and that is not for sale."

8. *A minister must not encroach upon the field of another*

[7] "A minister should be scrupulously careful in giving indorsements to agencies or individuals unless he has a thorough knowledge and approval of their work lest such indorsements be used to influence others unduly." (*Presbyterian Code*, III, 6.)

profession. Fortunately there is little danger of anything of this sort becoming widespread, though the great interest in pastoral psychology and its relationship to psychiatry and certain types of mental and moral involvement has drawn pastors and psychiatrists into overlapping territory in certain instances. Much more might be said regarding this, but it suffices to say that both the physician and the minister should know where the work of one stops, and that of the other begins.

There have been a few instances in which the minister attempted to prescribe for his people's physical ills. However, even in the few cases where the D.D. is also an M.D., let medical ethics be observed, if not ministerial, and the case left to the attending physician. Needless to say, any criticism of a doctor's treatment of a patient should not be indulged in by a minister. Some have made trouble for themselves by acting as self-constituted physicians or nurses. Of course in emergencies where medical attention of a simple sort is required, the minister, like any other man, will apply first aid and do what he can.

9. *The minister must not lower his profession by becoming a "handy man" for all the members of his church.* One pastor was kind enough to assist certain families a few times with the use of his automobile. It soon became the usual thing for the people to call for him whenever someone had to be taken to the hospital in the near-by city, or to visit the dentist there. Sometimes he was telephoned and asked to meet some member of one of the families of the church coming in on a night train, and it was explained that the family found it "inconvenient" to be there. Now "I serve" is the minister's motto, and no matter how humble the task, the minister ought to be willing to do it for the Master's sake; but the pastor who thus becomes a hewer of wood and a drawer of water for his people will not only find himself endlessly taxed along this line, but his own standing as

a proclaimer of gospel truth will become obscured. Where there is need, of course, work must be done, no matter how menial; but the people should learn that there is a higher duty devolving upon the minister than to act as errand boy for the community.

10. *The minister must hold his professional service in such esteem that he will keep it from being dissipated in the maze of shallow channels of service which open out in all directions today.* He is visited, for instance, by a person who wishes to arrange for a cultural and educational program to be given in the community and for the school children. The minister is asked to take the lead in this and "put it over." It is argued that the planned cultural affair will bring an enlarged vision to the community and to the children; it will teach new lessons, inculcate new ideals, and lay a wonderful foundation for spiritual growth; it will be a magnificent opportunity for the minister to show himself public-spirited and at the same time help along his own work. Will he not therefore accept the responsibility for the success of the program?

All of the above is true, for the sake of argument, but why not ask the minister to teach school? That, too, is a good work, noble work. Why not ask him to sell good books or distribute high-class magazines? These will build up knowledge among his people. Why not ask him to go out and stand all night with the policeman and see that the law is properly respected and enforced? That is a vastly important work. In short, why not ask him to do any and every good job that is to be done in his town or community? Why not? Simply because he is not called to any of these things, noble as they are. He is called to preach the unsearchable riches of Christ Jesus, and anything less than this cometh of evil. Not that he cannot and should not become all things to all men, for he can; and at times he must lead in certain undertakings. Not that he should not be a supporter of the cultural program and the school and the policeman, just as is any other good citizen. By reason of his training and talents he has a higher obligation toward certain forms of voluntary public social service than has the ordinary man. But let the minister recognize and show forth for all time and eternity, by his every word and act, that the place he occupies and the position he fills are unique in a peculiar way. He has a distinctive work all his own. No one can compete with him in his own field, nor may he compete with others without loss to himself. Let him know that and show that. Let him write it on his mind and heart. Let him eschew all sidetracks that lead off the main highway. Let him confine all his energies to his own great mission—and he will be rewarded by doing well that peculiar work to which the Lord his God has called him.

CHAPTER II

The Minister as a Man

A remarkable characteristic distinguishes the Christian ministry from every other profession. This characteristic was perhaps best stated in an address given by President Woodrow Wilson to a band of Christian workers and ministers in New York upon one occasion. The President, declaring the thought and teaching of his own father along this line, said that the Christian minister must *be* something before he can *do* anything. That is, his character and person are greater than his work—or rather, his work depends on his personal character. This is not true of other professions. It does not matter, for instance, what sort of character a lawyer may have; the jury looks at the facts and the evidence he brings out in each particular case. It does not matter what sort of man a doctor is if he is a "good doctor." But the minister as a person stands above his work, his sermon, his all. His preaching is measured by what the people know of the man; his work is tested by the character he shows. He may have the tongue of a Demosthenes and the executive ability of a Richelieu; but if he is not personally known to be a good servant of Jesus Christ, neither oratory nor ability will avail.

This is a vastly important conception for every minister to have. President Wilson was right—the old Presbyterian preacher of Staunton had got to the bottom of things. After a minister is what God will have him be, he will forthwith do what God would have him do.

So every preacher stands on the shoulders of the man he really is. He lives among his people; he has public and private meetings with them; and his life comes to be known and read of all. For him there is no awesome seclusion to heighten the sense of his dignity. He has no control over mystic or awe-inspiring symbols, as had the priests of other times. The people see the man himself standing clear of all the wrappings of ministerial cloth. Wherefore it has come to be that by so much as his character is known, by that much is his strength measured—for good or ill. Because the people know the man, they listen to the preacher; because they see him as a neighbor, they respect him as pastor. What he does speaks louder than what he says. As expressed before, primarily he must *be* something.

The man therefore, who is the minister, has certain duties to himself and to his person. There are obligations he owes to himself and to his own manhood, and these it is our purpose to observe and catalogue in this chapter. Some of these duties are obvious and may be dismissed with a bare mention; others are matters that require a brief discussion.

Physical life

A prime duty for every person is *proper care of the body*. The minister will preach only as long as his physical body is a functioning organism in this world. He will preach well, or serve well, only when his body, the physical nexus of his soul and the universe, functions well. Thought along this line is too trite to follow, nor may we go into a discussion as to ways and means of "keeping fit," with side notes on "How to prevent preacher's sore throat," or "Why ministers break down at fifty," or any of the matters involved in this question. That the minister owes some time and thought to his body is conceded by all, but the pity is that the minister will recognize the common sense of this statement, agree to the entire list of obligations which he owes himself in the line of recreation and exercise, and then straightway go and forget what manner of man he is. Too many ignore the whole physical basis of life and reap as a result collapse in middle life, or are handicapped for their remaining years by some personal disability. The remedy here is to face this obligation squarely and, come what may, work out some plan whereby physical exercise is taken on a rigorous schedule.[1]

A certain definite time for *rest and recreation* in connection with the ordinary routine of ministerial life and labor ought to be set aside deliberately—such is the prevailing opinion among ministers. Of course every minister holds himself ready to spend and be spent. In extraordinary emergencies he will go without sleep or rest—not to mention recreation. However, one day a week he may reasonably plan to use for his own relaxation and rest, as other professional men and workers should also do. Sunday is the preacher's working day; therefore some other day must be his day of rest. Monday was formerly regarded as the minister's "day off," and many choose it as such now; but the majority of the ministerial authorities relied on by this book indicate that Monday is no longer the most popular professional rest day. Many choose Saturday, some take Tuesday, and quite a few combine Monday morning and Saturday afternoon into

---

[1] "It is the minister's duty to keep himself in as good physical condition as possible." (*Unitarian Code*, I, 4.)

"It is equally the minister's duty to keep physically fit. A weekly holiday and an annual vacation should be taken and used for rest and improvement." (*Congregational Code*, I, 3. *Methodist* and *Presbyterian Codes* identical.)

"I will endeavor to keep physically and emotionally fit for my work." (*Disciples Code*, I.)

a sort of ministerial *sabbatismos*. One distinguished minister states that he prefers to work steadily for three or four weeks at a time, and then go away from his parish for two to four days in order to rest and refit himself for work again. This whole matter is one for the individual to settle according to personal needs, as many ministers insist when queried regarding it. A number of our authorities feel that the pursuit of some hobby, even at irregular intervals and with no daily recreational schedule, will often take the place of a regular "rest day." Of hobbies it may be said that while they tyrannize over those who adopt them (and are always looked at askance by others), they do have a balancing effect upon life as a whole.

One positive affirmation can be made about ministerial recreation: it should be entirely unlike the routine work of the week or it will not serve as recreation. If mental labor and the study of books, the visiting of the sick and the comforting of those in trouble is a man's life work, then let him beware of spending his leisure in writing articles or "paying helpful calls," even though these may be agreeable pastimes. The postman should not take a walk on his holiday, and the minister should not study on his if he wishes the day to achieve its proper results. The golf links or the highway, the drive to isolated places, the stream or shore, the workbench in the cellar—at any place or in any way that suits him, the minister should rejoice in the liberty in which God gives him a chance to be free one day in seven.

The Monday morning *ministers' meeting* has come to be an institution in many places, but this has not of late years seemed to enjoy the popularity which once it had. Present-day ministers feel that such meetings are too much like a continuation of their own regimen, the programs too fixed and routine. Most authorities consulted state that they do not attend such gatherings. "They make me gloomy"; are "seldom helpful"; "a waste of time," certain prominent ministers comment.

But there are others who find these meetings very helpful and all agree that the fellowship they provide is desirable to a high degree. "A man should help make these meetings what they ought to be. It is unwise for the stronger ministers to get bored and cease to attend," writes one man who is among the "stronger" ministers himself. It is a truism that young ministers are more quickly integrated with the ministerial brotherhood by attending these meetings regularly than in any other way. The objective here would seem to be watchfulness on the part of ministerial associations to see that their programs offer true inspiration and fellowship rather than a continuation of the regimen that has bound the minister all week. Heavy educational courses often tried by local ministerial associations destroy the spirit of freedom that should prevail. Ministers like to talk to each other, and are profoundly interested in each other. To that extent they very much enjoy getting together. Of course there may be need for definite group action by ministerial associations, and it will sometimes be necessary to make a business session out of the ministers' meeting. As a rule, however, business sessions ought to be called for that definite purpose, and not take up the fellowship hour of the members. The minister's day of rest should be his own. It will not always be so, of course, for funerals, deaths, sickness, or other duties that cannot be put off will press in upon his day of rest—but sufficient unto the day is the evil thereof.[2]

An *annual vacation period* is practically a necessity in present-day life, for the minister as well as for all other persons. This view

---

[2] "A weekly holiday and an annual vacation should be taken and used for rest and improvement." (*Congregational Code*, I, 3. *Methodist* and *Presbyterian Codes* identical.)

was not generally held by the ministers of seventy-five or a hundred years ago, some of whom argued that the devil never took a holiday so why should they? But that school of thought has passed away—perhaps because its adherents followed their theory too closely. It is recognized now that "there is that scattereth, and yet increaseth." Ministers everywhere hold that vacation is not an attempt to flee duty, but to be all the more ready for duty. Just as the Master's "Come . . . apart . . . and rest awhile" called his own away that they might refit themselves for service amid the "still dews of quietness," and "calm of hills above," so his modern disciples feel that for them, too, there should be occasional periods of calm in which they may "rest awhile."

The length of the annual vacation as well as the type desired varies greatly among American ministers. In the North and Northeast, vacations are quite often from six weeks to two months or even more in length. Over the South and West a month is the standard length of such vacations, and the vast majority of the authorities furnishing data for this book stated that a month is the usual vacation period. Most ministers seem to feel that a month provides an equitable measure of time off, though many hold that two months or more would not be too long. It should be said for the ministers who are given a long vacation that these men use part of this time quite definitely for ministerial work—planning sermons, catching up on needed reading, and the like.

Preaching in some other pulpit during the vacation may prove unwise, though quite often the opportunity for new fellowship and the nonburdensome work of preaching a familiar and well-tried message may give a certain reflex inspiration to the minister on its own account.

Certain ministers report that they manage to divide their vacation opportunities so that a Sunday, perhaps a week or ten days, is available to them in the winter as well as a somewhat longer summer period. But one able authority advises definitely against dividing vacation time. "It is better as a rule to take the weeks of one's vacation together. In this way they have a cumulative power."

In all fairness the matter of the length of a minister's vacation should be faced from the church's point of view as well as the minister's. Any church loses traction when its pastor is away from his people for many Sundays, and it always takes longer to pick up in the fall after a pastorless summer period. Furthermore there has been increasing concern of late years among substantial loyal laymen who feel that their church's program is practically at a standstill for the long summer period. This concern is accentuated, no doubt, because the rank and file of the membership have only a two-week vacation themselves.

Mental life

An essential ministerial duty is the *cultivation of the mind* and the corresponding improvement of professional and spiritual powers by application and study. Long ago William G. T. Shedd said that the holiest men have been the most studious. Even John Wesley, who was jealous of every moment of time both for himself and his preachers, gave the strictest injunctions to his not always educated men as to the duty of studying and reading. Wesley insisted:

Read the most useful books, and that regularly and constantly. Steadily spend all the morning in this employ, or, at least, five hours in four-and-twenty.

"But I read only the Bible."

Then you ought to teach others to read only the Bible, and, by parity of reason, to hear only the Bible: but if so, you need preach no more. . . . If you need no book but the Bible, you are got above St. Paul. He wanted others too. . . .

"But I have no taste for reading."

Contract a taste for it by use, or return to your trade.[3]

The artist has a "studio," the businessman an "office"; the preacher should have a *study*. Indeed since early days that room in which the minister lives, or is supposed to live, with his books has been known by the title just given—the study. Today, to be sure, since the minister must often act as a business executive, many churches have frankly adopted the term "office" for the room in which the church staff functions. But for the place where the minister can have privacy and prepare for his own distinctive work, we prefer the old name and old ideal.

This may be a room in the parsonage, manse, or rectory if due quiet can be secured there. It may be a room in the church, and the larger churches usually provide a study as part of their equipment. However, due to the frequent calls and interruptions which come to the usual city minister—especially when he is known to be at the church—many men secure needed privacy by seeking a more secluded room or retreat during their study hours. There they may be reached in case of an emergency by the few who know their whereabouts, but on normal mornings they find it wise to put themselves beyond the reach of the telephone or casual callers.

Ministers seldom have the opportunity to say much about the lighting and other appointments of the study the church provides for them. A light, cheerful room is, of course, preferable. "Don't let them give you a study with stained-glass windows in

[3] "Minutes of Several Conversations between the Rev. Mr. Wesley and others, from the year 1744 to 1789"; Question 32.

41

it," a bishop once advised his preachers, "or you will have a gloom cast over all your thinking. Get some light and air."

The chief *study faults* to be guarded against are too much specialized study, or a bookishness which may result in taking one out of touch with life and its realities, and on the other hand—and this is the more common fault in our activistic ministerial life—too little study. This last is peculiarly a temptation of the present age, since the minister in many instances is expected to be more of a social engineer than a student, more the aggressive leader of a large congregation than a cloistered scholar. Let the bookish type give himself more to executive and pastoral work, and let every man study and read systematically in other fields than those which his special interests and training incline him to follow. "Grooved thinking" results in grooved preaching and in emphasizing continuously one particular aspect of Christian truth to the exclusion of others. The preacher himself seldom realizes how typed he can become by following, albeit unconsciously, some one subject in which he is particularly interested. Unfortunately what the minister does not realize his congregation soon does.

On the other hand the executive type of minister who delights to express himself in planning and promotion, and in the driving through of an activistic program, needs to take more time for the reading of books and the well-balanced study of the Christian ages. With all the activities and enterprises which a present-day minister is expected to carry on, there is yet in the minds of the people the feeling that the chief duty of a preacher is to preach. "How acceptable will a minister in your church be if he devotes the major portion of his time to preparing sermons?" asked Murray H. Leiffer of over a thousand influential laymen. In his book *The Layman Looks at the Minister* he reports that 60 per cent indicated that this emphasis would be desirable; 10

per cent were indifferent; while 30 per cent dissented. There was a strong lay condemnation of any minister who "fails to spend adequate time in his study."

Time and *system* must regulate ministerial habits of study as well as everything else. The morning hours are voted by all as best for close application and brain work, and those ministers whose judgment is relied upon by this book uniformly agree that the early part of the morning provides the best time of all. However, the great majority assert that the entire morning should be kept free for study if at all possible, though the time actually secured for this varies with different ministers. "Four hours, six days a week," proudly reports one successful pastor who has earned a name for himself as an able administrator as well as an able preacher. The average time secured by the average minister is somewhere around three hours a day.

A large number of ministers state that they prefer night hours as their time for professional study, though with others this period is mentioned as the occasion when they engage in general or nonprofessional reading. General reading is of professional help, in that it keeps a man in touch with the thought of the day and with the thinking of his people; but the vast majority of present-day ministers confess that they have to "catch as catch can" on time for such reading.

A large and often cumbersome *ministerial library* was practically essential fifty or seventy-five years ago, when the minister was isolated from library facilities and the cultural advantages now found in every town and city. Then the minister's study was the only place where he might arm himself for sermonic conquest, and he found it essential to have about him the books which actually were the tools of his trade. As a consequence there grew the large, well-furnished personal library. In fact a minister felt himself to be judged—and perhaps he was—by the books which lined his shelves. But times have somewhat changed. While the need of study is today even more pressing than in former days, modern advantages allow a certain streamlining of the over-booked library. The minister now knows that no matter how much time and money he spends in building a home library, he will have no great trouble in finding access to the books he needs in near-by places. Nearly every town of any size has a public library and with the coming of radio and television there are cultural advantages even in isolated places. As a consequence there has grown among ministers the idea of maintaining a working library—one that is adequate but not cumbersome. It should be chosen carefully for use, and not be merely a collection of impressive-looking books; it should be usable and not simply ornamental. There is, of course, no objection to the gathering of books as such when these can be secured by people who love them—as most of us do—and there are basic books which every minister must have as his own. But many good ministers affirm that for practical purposes there should be a quick turnover of the ephemeral book, with its place filled by another of its kind or by one of the volumes which are timeless in their proven value.

A working library will, of course, have the desk books, Bible, Testament, commentaries; at arm's reach, lexicon, encyclopedias, books of classic devotion, besides Prayer Book, Directory, Discipline, or whatever may be appropriate for one's own denomination. There are all manner of rich and helpful volumes with which a man may surround himself. A study of the reading habits of ministers published in *Publisher's Weekly* (June 21, 1941) brought out the fact that those with the heaviest duties bought and read the most books.[4]

[4] "The minister should count it a most important part of his work to keep in touch with the best religious thought of his day, and should make it a point

Spiritual life and duty

Absolutely primary to his calling and work is a minister's personal duty to cultivate his own spiritual life. Present-day ministers have discarded some of the techniques of the past, but in insisting upon this transcendent duty they are at one with the Christians of all the ages. Ministers are instinctively more alert upon this matter since they recognize a powerful but subtle temptation which their very life presents to them—that since they give all their time to the work of God they may be excused from setting aside one special portion of it for the expression of personal allegiance. But danger lies here. "They made me the keeper of the vineyards; but mine own vineyard have I not kept," was the startling text with which a well-known American preacher addressed a gathering of his fellow ministers. And while many of them knew that the Song of Solomon from which he took this text was probably saying something other than what he made of it, they knew also that he was saying something which needed to be said directly to them.

A man's very familiarity with sacred things may breed, not contempt, but spiritual obtuseness. The Bible becomes a quarry out of which to dig texts, not a reservoir for personal spiritual refreshment; prayer is something done for others, not for oneself; the lives of the saints, the rich devotional writings of Thomas à Kempis, Lancelot Andrewes, and the classic worthies of the past become sermonic material with which to stir others, not the heart throbs out of which life may be made; and we become—

of honor to set aside sufficient time for reading and study." (*Unitarian Code*, I, 3.)

"Part of the minister's service as the leader of his people is to reserve sufficient time for serious study in order thoroughly to apprehend his message, keep abreast of current thought, and develop his intellectual and spiritual capacities." (*Congregational Code*, I, 2. *Presbyterian* and *Methodist Codes* identical.)

God forgive us—professional. The quiet hour, prayer, the rigid discipline which we should like to see carried on by others should be undertaken by the minister himself if he is to be the man God would have him be.

Most present-day ministers indicate that they take the first hour of the morning for their own personal devotions. Practically all insist that the need here can only be met by an unbending purpose. "Be rigorous," urges one; "Work at it"; "Don't leave it to chance," insist others; while "disciplined prayer" and "a definite period invariably kept" sum up the advice of all. One of our authorities does confess that to him it never has been satisfactory to fix a special period for devotions, and another states that wherever he goes throughout the day he likes to feel it possible to withdraw within himself and commune with God. But all others insistently urge a special time and a definite regimen of devotion. Beside prayer and scripture, manuals of devotion and the like, one minister suggests a return to the almost lost art of meditation. All agree that no one can fulfill his ministry unless he keeps the fountains of his own spiritual life springing up afresh each day.[5]

Duties to home and family

Foremost among the duties of a minister are those he owes to his home and family. This is universally conceded, but too often the minister's home is immolated upon the altar of his work. The pastor has a hard task, but the pastor's family often has a harder one. Of course circumstances must again be taken into account in judging a possible conflict of duties here. There are times when an emergency in the home demands every thought of the father or husband; there are times when an emergency in the

---

[5] "I will cultivate my devotional life, continuing steadfastly in reading the Bible, meditation and prayer." (*Disciples Code*, I.)

church becomes so imperative that it takes precedence over all home duties. This will be admitted. What is not so easily remembered, however, is that a minister's relationship to his family is as high and as sacred as that to his church.

Happily there is usually no conflict here, but on the contrary a most beautiful interlocking of work and duties. The better the father, the better the pastor; the better the guide for the children of others, the better the guide for one's own children. Conflicts of course occur, and two situations in particular may cause difficulty.

First, the minister owes it to his family to make a living for them. If he does not, someone else—relatives or the community at large—will have to. His family must look to him and to him alone for food and clothing. "If I can't make a living for my wife in the ministry, I will resign and work where I can," a minister once said. He was not thinking of a luxurious living, nor of life in terms of money. What he meant was that if he should ever be faced with the fact that his wife and children needed food and raiment which he could not supply as long as he served as pastor, in that hard case the obligation of husband and father would supersede temporarily the obligation as pastor and preacher. There are many pastorates and many church members, but only one home. Many look to the minister as spiritual father, but only a definite few—and these few exceedingly precious—look to him as an earthly father. Neither the minister nor his family measures life in terms of the monthly pay check signed by the church treasurer; but no father, minister or otherwise, can forget those who look to him for daily bread.

It might be added that while a minister may not be able to give his family wealth or luxury, yet he can and should labor to make a comfortable, happy home for his children. The record of the ministers of the nation along this line is a proud one. The high percentage of successful men who have come from homes of ministers speaks not only of necessities supplied, but of industry, frugality, and a stimulating mental and spiritual atmosphere about the parsonage, rectory or manse. It is a noteworthy fact that in *Who's Who* there are more sons of ministers than of any other profession.

Second, the family of the minister should not be made to serve as slaves of the church, nor should their home be used as a public convenience for the entire membership. "Don't let ministerial life and domestic life get mixed," Lloyd C. Douglas wisely counseled in *The Minister's Everyday Life*. The minister's family, like any other in the congregation, ought to take an active part in the work of the church and its several departments. However, to force the wife into the position of assistant pastor and the children into becoming prodigies of childish ecclesiastical leadership is wrong. It is not fair to the family and it spoils the church.[6]

All things being equal, the family of the minister should have the same rights and privileges, duties and obligations that belong to other Christian families. Of course it is recognized that the family in the parsonage should be a model family—but so should every home circle be. The reputation which ministers' children bear either for good or for ill is usually not of their own making. They are credited as being much better than the ordinary run of children until it is found that they are not; then they are accused of being much worse than they really are. But wisdom is justified of all her children—including those of ministers.

A book of its own might be written about the *minister's wife*, and indeed several such books have been written. It is sufficient

---

[6] "I will be fair to my family and will endeavor to give them the time and consideration to which they are entitled." (*Disciples Code*, I.)

here to say—to ministers, not primarily to their wives—that no matter what role the congregation expects her to play, the minister very properly sees his wife as *his* wife, to love and to cherish, to protect and to support. He must not forget that she married him, not a whole congregation—at least that is what she thought she was doing. As Bess White Cochran states in describing her mother, a minister's wife:

All ministers' wives have a tremendously delicate job. Few of them probably choose such a calling deliberately. They fall in love with a dreaming youth—and there they are. But all who bear this kinship with the ministry are confronted with a peculiar opportunity. The world looks at them a little askance, and yet a little hopefully.[7]

In the matter of church work the minister's wife may be expected to give what time and attention she can to helpful service, just as any other Christian woman does. If she has unusual talent or ability, let her use her talent as any Christian should. But ministers' wives who have dramatized their own abilities have not always been the help to their husbands that they fancied they were. The greatest and most successful pastors and preachers have usually been supported—not supplanted—by a wife to whom they and the congregation were in debt in ways which can never be properly appreciated or known. Even were it possible for the minister's wife to be a paragon in both home and church, it is not certain that the general life of the church would be too greatly helped. When the next minister comes along, his wife may be an invalid, or have a baby, or be incapable of outside leadership; and it will count heavily against her if the congregation has the idea that a minister's wife should be a combination

[7] *I Married a Minister*, ed. Golda Elam Bader (used by permission of Abingdon-Cokesbury Press).

Sunday school teacher, social service worker, playground director, junior church superintendent, and sick nurse.

Mrs. Cochran, telling of her mother's attitude toward this situation, says:

Mother . . . never held on to the office of president of the Ladies Aid or the missionary society or to any position of prominence too long. She would take her turn along with the rest, but she considered part of her job was to help her husband develop the latent leadership that was all too content to warm the church pews or coach from the side lines. Similarly, although she was blessed with a fine alto voice and often sang in the church choir, she never allowed any director or music committee to make her a soloist. Her voice was pleasing, and sounded to us like an angel's, but she knew that its too frequent use in the choir loft could cause disquieting reverberations in the pews.

I never saw my mother at church suppers peeling potatoes when she should have been sitting beside her husband with the guest speaker. She didn't mind peeling potatoes, and even onions, and did her share of it; but as the wife of the minister she knew that something more was expected of her than the ability to work tirelessly in the kitchen.

Personal finances

There is one inflexible duty which the minister owes to himself, to his family, to his profession, and to his church—he must be absolutely exact on money matters. "Financial looseness or irregularity cannot be tolerated," Washington Gladden observed long ago. All the preaching a man may do will not atone for unpaid bills. He may have what is to him a good excuse, but in the eyes of the world there is no excuse for failure to pay debts.

In this connection something may be added concerning extravagance, or incurring debts without the strong probability of paying them. Every man can make mistakes along this line, but the minister should be very careful whenever he incurs any obligation that will be for him unusually heavy.[8]

In former days a great many things were given to the minister, and he was often the recipient of goods and provisions in lieu of money, as well as of the *ministerial discount*. The United States was then a rural, agrarian nation where money was scarce and where the minister—and the physician as well—was often paid "in kind." To "have something ready for the preacher" or to sell him goods at reduced rates became customary in early American life. But those days are gone and "clergy discount," as a survey shows, is not the common practice that it was thirty years ago, and is unknown in certain places. Nevertheless in almost every region there are stores and mercantile establishments where the practice is continued. The question is, What to do about it?

A small but quite influential number of ministers take the position that such favors really are a detriment to a minister's work. They argue that gratuities and discounts destroy self-respect, and that the people who offer them have a tendency to feel that they have been relieved of deeper spiritual obligations. "Let the minister be paid a wage commensurate with his work and standing," observed one well-known clergyman; "then he will neither need nor should he take such supposed favors."

But to the direct question as to whether the acceptance of ministerial discount is embarrassing, the great majority of our ministerial authorities said, "No." Specifically, 77 per cent affirm that their policy is to accept such discount when it is tendered;

[8] "The minister should set a high moral standard of speech and conduct. He should be scrupulous in the prompt payment of bills, and careful in the incurring of financial obligations." (*Unitarian Code*, I, 5.)

"As an ethical leader in the community, it is incumbent on the minister to be scrupulously honest, avoid debts, and meet his bills promptly." (*Congregational Code*, I, 6. *Methodist* and *Presbyterian Codes* identical.)

23 per cent say that such discount should be courteously refused.

An inquiry as to whether physicians in various sections of the country charge ministers for their professional services, or make a nominal charge or no charge at all, elicited the information that the custom in this regard varies with different physicians. Some charge full rates, while others will not hear of receiving anything from the minister. When the doctor is a member of the minister's church this is usually the case and there is often a tie between physician and pastor that transcends financial considerations. In fact the spirit in which ministerial discount is tendered largely determines whether or not the minister should accept it. There are some courtesies so offered that they cannot be refused without offending. For example, when a splendid Maryland doctor declined to charge a minister for his services, the minister insisted rather unpleasantly on receiving a statement, as he "liked to pay his bills." The doctor answered quietly that he was not showing a favor to the minister personally, but to the calling he represented. He added that as a doctor he did not have the opportunity to serve God as the minister could, but that his medical service was an avenue that God opened to him, and that it was his pleasure thus to serve. What minister could have done other than accept after that?

This generous attitude, even though it is passing, represents the other side of this debatable question of ministerial discount. When a favor is granted as a mark of honor and respect to the profession, the individual minister usually takes it as such, and not as a private favor. The minister is, after all, the recipient of favors and even gratuities because he *is* the minister. Sometimes he does not like it; and the drift of thought among present-day ministers is that the ministerial profession should be paid like other professions and that there should be no more gratuities. On the whole this is well, but something priceless may be lost when pastoral services are to be paid for entirely in terms of cash. The minister will then, of course, be more independent, but so will the people—and God help a church whose pastor is independent of the people and the people of the pastor.

On the other hand where he knows that he will be the recipient of a special favor—that the physician will not charge him, the storekeeper will let him have goods "at cost"—the self-respecting clergyman is apt to go without the medical service that another man would instantly summon, and will shun the storekeeper lest he seem to be begging a favor. This is a strong argument against receiving any gratuities and discounts.

In general it would seem better, where no pastoral tie is involved, for the minister to pay his bills like any other man if he may do so without offending. And when the physician makes no charge, thoughtful ministers see to it that the doctor in question is remembered by a substantial present on such occasions as Christmas or his birthday.

Unfortunately it is true that there are some pastors who presume on the ministerial discount, on the free medical attention. One such minister can do more harm than all the men who quietly go to other stores rather than appear where they know they will be given a discount. But it is a sad fact that because ministers are often given considerations which other men do not receive, some of them unconsciously get into the attitude of mind which expects these considerations. Such men show their disappointment—and talk of it—when no special favor is given them; and when one is given, they take it simply as a matter of course. Some have grown old in this habit of mind, and it is bad, very bad.[9]

Upon the matter of the *clergy fare*, or the reduced rate which the American railroads usually allow to ministers, there is more

[9] "I will not seek special gratuities." (*Disciples Code*, II.)

53

unanimity of clerical opinion. Only three of our authorities state that they refuse to take advantage of the clergy rate; seven say that they use it for church business only. All others replying state that they use or approve the use of the clergy fare. It is significant that many of the great denominational and interdenominational boards, commissions, councils, and agencies frankly advise use of the clergy fare for necessary travel to their gatherings, and sometimes the allowance for ecclesiastical travel expense is based on such reduced fare.

What to do about *fees* tendered the minister for certain services has proved even more troublesome than clergy discount. There is more variety of opinion and of practice among the clergy on this matter of fees than in almost anything else. Here again there are those who insist that the answer would be found if a proper salary were to be paid each minister "with no emoluments." As it is, the wedding fee, which has long been a traditional and welcome visitor to the parsonage or manse, seems destined to continue. Sixty-one of our authorities say they accept wedding fees; five report that they do not. But fees for baptism—which are in truth rather rare—are not accepted. Twenty-three will accept funeral fees; thirty-five will not, though in the matter of funeral fees there are all sorts of qualifying stipulations presented. Many ministers state that when they do accept funeral fees they put them in some special fund and let it be understood that such a course is being followed; others affirm, and very properly, that where the minister has been put to personal expense in connection with a funeral, as in traveling to a distant place, it is entirely proper to accept remuneration for such expenses. Some call attention to the fact that people in deep sorrow may be hurt if their kindly meant enclosure is not taken, and that "it takes great tact to know how to do." It does —and not only at funerals.

Certain ministers state that they refuse to accept any fees, even wedding fees, from their own members. They say that their pastoral relationship to their members precludes such acceptance. They will, however, accept fees from outsiders—that is, from those who have no claim on them. On the other hand there are ministers who say that they always refuse fees from outsiders lest they give the impression that ministerial service is something which can be bought with a price. This last group, however, is not a large one; and most ministers feel that where people have no real claim upon the church, the minister may more readily accept from them such fees as may be tendered. Dr. Raymond Calkins, treating of this whole matter, states, "I feel that the higher ethics of the profession call for the declination of fees for personal use. If accepted, it should be made plain that they will be used for charity."

Summing up the consensus of ministerial judgment: wedding fees are to be accepted; baptismal fees, being rare, present no problem; funeral fees are not to be accepted unless refusal makes for unpleasantness and embarrassment. When such fees are accepted, let them be put in a special fund or used for some worthy cause.[10]

[10] "Professional service should be gladly rendered to all, without regard to compensation, except for necessary expenses incurred." (*Unitarian Code*, III, 4.)

CHAPTER III

The Minister as a Citizen

We now come to a vexed question—the minister's relation to civic and national affairs. He is a citizen of the state like any other American, and enjoys all the rights and privileges appertaining to citizenship; and yet, since he is the representative of a spiritual kingdom which, as he preaches, is not of this world, a strange dual relationship faces him. How much citizen of the world is he? How much priest of God?

It would be impossible if not wrong for the minister to refuse to face the implications of his own citizenship. He is, in fact, one of the civic leaders wherever he lives. He, with the judge, the doctor, and the schoolteacher, is more to the fore on the local stage than is the ordinary citizen whose vocation does not so hold him before the public. In addition to this the minister is known as one who can make a speech, and so is called upon frequently for addresses outside his own pulpit. In his own church it is his privilege and duty to address a public audience twice every week. This in itself would be enough to make him a force in the local community and more or less a leader in civic affairs.

Now comes the question: How large a part in local affairs, in national affairs, shall the minister take? If he might appear as an ordinary man, the now complicated question of his relation to public affairs would not exist. He would, like any other man, stand or fall with his own ideas, his own party. But whether he wishes it or not, by virtue of his position he is not an ordinary citizen. His utterances are not only given in public—they are seized upon by both press and people as weighty words. It is true that he, with the schoolteacher, doctor, and others, stands on a local pedestal; but his words are commonly taken as of far more importance than are the utterances of these other local citizens. This is because he is looked upon as an ambassador of God, and all that he may say or do in an attempt to divest himself of this ministerial character and appear as an ordinary citizen somehow fails. How, then, shall this combination man, this citizen-minister or minister-citizen, act? What things are Caesar's and what things are God's? That is our question in this chapter.

Civic service

The minister, representing the Church, is often called upon for public addresses, public prayer, etc., in civic and national assemblies. Few formal secular programs are deemed complete without an invocation and sometimes a benediction by a Christian minister. Our legislative assemblies are opened with a prayer by a chaplain, and so are some courts; the government provides for chaplains with the armed forces of the nation and in such places as prisons and hospitals. The minister who is placed in such a situation will find that the course of conduct governing his actions is somewhat different from the usual pulpit and parish procedure.

He should realize, first, that he is placed in public nonecclesiastical assemblies—for instance, to open a public gathering with prayer—by virtue of the fact that he represents the entire Christian ministry and not one special branch of it. Hence it is axiomatic with every minister so situated to represent as best he can the whole Christian Church. By no word or deed does he give even a faint suggestion that he may be taking advantage of the occasion for denominational purposes.

Rarely has a minister so placed transgressed this unwritten rule. The usual minister is well aware of this general representative character, and so proud to be the mouthpiece of the Universal Church that he is extremely anxious to act for all the forces which he feels to be sustaining him. The chaplain of the state senate or house, the chaplain of the prison, the chaplain of the regiment, never forgets the broadness of his service. If the truth be told, these men usually "lean over backward" in order to be impartial. Stories come to us from the war telling how Christian chaplains ministered to the dying Jewish soldier in the name of a common God, and how Jewish rabbis held up the cross before the eyes of the dying Catholic. Under the triphammer of war our little denominational symbols, whether of sand or clay or stone, were alike crushed to atoms.

When a minister is called upon for any public address, as upon Thanksgiving Day, school commencement, or other occasion, he acts in accordance with the principle just set forth. Such themes as are handled are general ones, appropriate to the nature of the occasion. Needless to say, one could scarcely afford to take advantage of such a situation for any private or denominational reasons. A breach of faith here would backfire with disastrous results.

Invocations at public meetings

Present-day ministers are somewhat divided on the matter of responding to the many calls that come to them for *invocations* at civic banquets, luncheon club meetings, and the like. Those who object state that such meetings are time-consuming, and the service the minister is asked to render is often viewed as a perfunctory formality. "The importance of such service is over-rated," avers a popular pastor in the capital city of a great state, while a midwestern minister says flatly, "If you are invited simply because people expect an invocation and there is no appreciation behind it—skip it."

But the majority of modern ministers see an opportunity here. They feel that even at the risk of losing time, invitations of any importance at all should be accepted. "The occasion must determine the decision," states a minister of wisdom and experience; "lesser affairs warrant a courteous negative to save time." Most agree that there is an opportunity for a representative Christian service, and that it is well to keep to the fore in civic life the old idea that the blessing of God is to be sought for any important undertaking or public convocation. "Accept the invitation if it is a decent affair," advises a distinguished Baptist leader. "You may do some good."

The stipulation just cited—"if it is a decent affair"—indicates a caution which must be observed whenever a minister is invited to have a place on a public program. Will his own appearance on the program be in keeping with his ministerial calling? Usually of course it will be; and any doubt at all can be cleared by understanding beforehand the exact nature of the occasion in which he is to be involved. The presence of the minister, and especially his participation in any public event, is viewed as an indorsement of whatever transpires. The cloth of the minister makes wonderful camouflage—and Mr. Worldly-Wiseman knows it.

The professional rule that under no circumstances may a minister forswear his ministerial calling or Christian character must be carefully observed on all public occasions. In the attempt to be a good fellow at the civic club luncheon there have been ministers whose stories and speeches were out of keeping with their profession. Such men lose far more than they gain and are marked down more than they realize by the very men they are trying to impress.

Interfaith meetings and the like sometimes put a Christian minister in a position where he finds the virtue of tolerance in conflict with the definite affirmations his calling represents. It was reported in Washington when a great international gathering, official in character, was being held, that the minister selected to open the assembly was cautioned against making the prayer a definitely Christian one and was requested not to close with the name of Jesus. The story is possibly not true, but the fact that the United Nations has not found it advisable to open sessions with Christian prayer lends some credence to a possible difficulty here.

But in response to the definite question: If asked to pray before an interfaith conference but cautioned to omit the usual ascription "in the name of Jesus" in order not to offend other religious groups, should the minister refuse the invitation or respect the request? Thirty-six of our ministerial authorities held that the request should be respected. Twenty-eight, on the other hand, believed the minister should refuse the invitation. Others either failed to reply or were indefinite. One hardy character said that he would do both—accept the invitation and "pray as a Christian." However, it would seem that the very nature of the Christian witness prevents the minister from abnegating his calling. If he may not appear as a minister of Christ, he should not appear at all.

When the issue becomes one of public prayer against entrenched social evil there is no uncertainty. Public prayer as a forensic act has sometimes caused political repercussions, and every minister knows it. In one state legislature the prayer of the chaplain caused objection among the opponents of the moral forces. He himself was finally waited upon by a committee and asked to be less explicit in his public petitions. At the same time he was reminded that his position was a political one, that political forces could remove him as they had made him. One may imagine how a delegation of this sort would fare at the hands of an Amos or a Jeremiah, but we have no sure knowledge of what transpired in the case above mentioned. Again it seems the part of Christian manhood to represent the Christian consciousness and only that, regardless of consequences. The minister cannot deny himself or his God. If public prayer before any audience is a ceremonial formula and that only, then why waste time—to make it no worse—in imitation of an awful act? If it be what it pretends to be, then, in God's name, there can be no trifling.

Privileges of citizenship

The minister has certain privileges, just as any other citizen does. He should register and comply with such regulations as enable him to vote. The only dispute that may be waged with this idea is brought by the man who says that politics are so rotten that the ministry should have nothing to do with them. This is sometimes heard from pious cranks on the one hand, and from political bosses, who are neither pious nor cranks, on the other. Dr. Washington Gladden once said in discussing the secularization of the pulpit that there are two classes who cry out against it—those who hold that religion has nothing to do with the world, and those who do not want to know what difference Christian applications may make in this field.[1] These two classes are the only ones who object to the minister's right to the ballot, and he does well to ignore such objections and be a citizen with the other citizens of his land.

[1] *The Christian Pastor and the Working Church.*

Besides the positive privileges such as the ballot and the inalienable rights to life, property, and protection which the minister enjoys with other men, he has certain ministerial privileges recognized by the state which it may be well to mention here. These may be termed negative privileges, since they are in the nature of immunities given the ministry by the civil power.

1. The minister is usually exempted from *jury duty*. This is an outgrowth of old English common law procedure which looked upon the *clerici* as men of mercy and not of judgment. It may be recalled that when a state trial takes place in the English House of Lords, the bishops, who are the ecclesiastical peers, always file out before a vote is taken, on the theory that the vote of the clergy must be for—certainly cannot be against—mercy. American practice follows English, and no minister in our land ever finds himself as talesman in a jury box, except perhaps in one or two states.

2. The minister is not summoned to *serve in the armed forces* in time of war. This is an exemption which Congress has always granted under its constitutional power to "raise armies and provide for the common defense." During the First World War certain clergymen affirmed that exemption from military duty was a slight upon the manhood of the ministry.[2] However, no objection of that sort was raised during the Second World War; and universal opinion, both clerical and lay, agrees that the state does well in refusing to put weapons of carnal warfare in the hands of the men of God. Even chaplains accepted by and serving with the armed forces are classed as noncombatants and by the laws of war cannot wear side arms or use weapons of any kind.

3. The state will not and cannot force the ministry to any

[2] *Literary Digest,* November 3, 1917.

service which violates conscience. It cannot compel a minister to marry a couple if he is unwilling; it cannot compel him to testify in court concerning confessions which may have been made to him in his pastoral capacity—with some exceptions.

It will be seen in the above that there is a recognition accorded the minister by the state which is not given to the ordinary citizen. These privileges he should recognize as belonging to the sacred nature of his office, and he should accept them accordingly. In turn the minister should pay back to his state his loyalty and his service in his distinctive way.[3]

Political and social questions

We now come to a critical and debatable question. What part should the church and minister take in shaping the social and political life of the community? Should the pastor actively engage in any movement for social or political betterment which will entangle him with local interests and persons? Should he speak from the pulpit on such matters? Some ministers and denominations answer, "Under no circumstances"; others reply, "In case a moral issue is involved"; still others, "Yes—on all matters that affect the life of the Church and her people."

Much has been written along this line. Usually one's findings are colored by traditional views. The older, more conservative ecclesiasticisms as a rule abhor the idea of using the church or pulpit in any ephemeral (to them) political conflict. On the other hand there are modern types who decry with scorn the minister who, leaving the issues of the living present, preaches on the sins of Abraham, Isaac, and Jacob, but never speaks

[3] "The minister's responsibility to the state is that of a citizen. He should, therefore, be faithful to his public obligations, and should respond to reasonable requests for assistance in community work." (*Unitarian Code*, V, 2.)

against local aldermanic tyranny or judicial partiality. In *The Wicket Gate* Studdert Kennedy said in his own vigorous style:

If the Church is to be a Church indeed, and not a mere farce—and a peculiarly pernicious farce, a game of sentimental make-believe—she must be filled to overflowing with the fire of the ancient prophets for social righteousness, with the wrath and love of the Christ.

More and more there is a demand for the Church to come to grips with present pressing problems, economic, social, political. The question is one of importance and men differ much in their opinions. Some never permit their ordered and stately worship to be interrupted by anything, no matter what social or political storm may be raging among the people. Others rush quickly into what are clearly partisan matters and thunder at local political conditions, at one party machine or the other. Quite often these men advocate from the pulpit cataclysmic measures, all under the sanction of religion. When, for instance, an industrial strike is on, such ministers take sides and preach on the strike, sometimes with violence and fury. As a consequence they earn from one side high plaudits, and from the other unqualified hate. Their apology—if they give one—is the idea above set forth: The Church should be a big factor in the life of today. Of what use is it, they say, to ignore the present pressing matters of bread and meat, right and wrong, human shame and degradation, and preach on hypothetical questions dead and done with these many centuries? Let the Church speak and rebuke evil wherever it is. Thus she fulfills her mission and thus she makes for righteousness.

When all is said there is no absolute ruling that can be made. Conditions vary and a speech or a sermon that might be an imprudence from one man may be the fulfilling of all righteousness when it comes from another. There are times when the minister of God must speak, let the political chips fall where they may.

Careful inquiry indicates that the consensus of opinion among ministers of the Christian churches will fall in line with the following broad principles or guides for conduct.

1. No minister should in public speech or sermon take part *in partisan politics* as such. He may and should cast his ballot as has been said, and if he is a personality of any force at all will have a very definite opinion on the matters at issue in every partisan election. But *as a minister* or *in the pulpit* he should not pronounce upon partisan questions. This same principle will cover his procedure in all conflicts of a social and industrial sort when no moral principle is at stake.

Some ministers endeavor to excuse their participation in factional matters on the ground that they are not appearing as ministers but as men. They are citizens; therefore they are acting as citizens and not as clergymen. This is a distinction, however, that the usual person can never get through his head. If he sees the Reverend Doctor Blank speaking, then it is the Reverend Doctor Blank he sees, and all affirmations on the part of the Reverend Doctor that he is now not the Reverend Doctor, but just plain John Blank saying what he thinks—all this means nothing to the man in the street. He feels if someone tossed a brick on top of plain John Blank that the Reverend Doctor Blank would feel it pretty keenly—and so he would.

A well-expressed protest against this type of reasoning was sent years ago to Dr. Alexander Whyte, the distinguished preacher of Scotland. Dr. Whyte had spoken out warmly and strongly on the Irish question then agitating his nation, and the notoriety he obtained by so doing stirred the elders of his church to remonstrance. Their reasoning is cogent and timeless in its implication:

> We think that he [Dr. Whyte] cannot take such a part without to a greater or less extent compromising the congregation; he cannot divest himself in public estimation of his representative character, or fail to do something towards clothing his personal political opinions with the authority which belongs to his office; and he has been invested with that character and office . . . for other objects and on other considerations than those of secular politics. No one would ever think of questioning your sacred right of individual opinion and of supporting that opinion by your vote, but we venture to submit to you that many considerations . . . point to the high expediency of our minister abstaining from identifying himself in so marked a manner as you have recently done with either side of any burning political controversy.[4]

2. The minister not only has the right but is obligated to speak upon *purely moral questions*, in the pulpit or out of it, be the political or social implications what they may. None may say him nay here. The morals of the people, the tides of the time as these touch his people's lives, on these he is the declared authority.

But how is one to know what is a moral issue? Moral questions sometimes have political implications, and politicial questions sometimes have moral implications. A moral issue may be involved only in a minor way in some tempest in a municipal teapot. A needed social reform may be the least of all the planks in a political platform, and perhaps even then may bear evidence of having been tacked on to "gain the church vote." The most untrustworthy persons morally may have made the greatest pledges and be the highest bidders for moral support. All

---

[4] *Church Management*, August, 1926.

these angles give one pause, and, as hinted before, the minister who permits himself to be drawn into such local issues will discover many queer political bedfellows.

In this difficulty it is a safe rule to learn the opinion and thought of other ministers and churches upon the matter at issue. If the moral sentiment of a great ecclesiasticism, of several of them, or of the vast bulk of Christian people declares a paramount moral issue to be locked up in a social, economic, or political campaign, then the minister usually feels that he has a right to declare his moral sense of the matter. But a minister who undertakes to decide as to the rights and wrongs of great political and social movements all by himself, or who carries on a single-handed and individual warfare, becomes a sort of ecclesiastical bushwhacker or private sniper carrying on unorganized warfare. When such a one is caught—and it is not hard to catch him—he gets the treatment meted out to snipers, and the place thereof knows him no more. This is not to say that the individual may not be right, or that the firebrand is not sometimes necessary to start the conflagration. It is to emphasize the risk of setting oneself up as judge of all morals, arbiter of all rights and wrongs. Common sense says it is better to move with the organization and to be guided by the consensus of Christian thought.

3. When a minister speaks or preaches on burning moral questions as wound up in political or other alignments he must *understand thoroughly every phase* of the situation. It should be remembered that he has constituted himself a judge, jury, and, as far as possible, an executioner. The town, the city, the nation, sitting as a higher court, is going to review his judgment. It will wish to see the evidence on which he based his decision. What are the briefs, pro and con? Has the side he adjudges wrong had a chance to present its case, if not in "open court" at least in

public? What was the defense? He has publicly found for the other side, and the world wants to know why. If a minister has based his decision on hearsay evidence, common report, or "what people say," he had best watch himself.

In connection with this there is a fault to which ministers are particularly prone. It might be treated in other places, but it comes in here very naturally. The ministry as a class is given to uttering generalities in a way that is dangerous. No one answers the minister from the pew nor subjects his running statements to careful scrutiny. Bishop Charles H. Brent, who usually knew what he was talking about, said:

The sermon is, by established custom, a monologue which the preacher delivers without fear of contradiction or interruption. . . . If the preacher, who is now protected by laws prohibiting any interruption of divine service, were to expect the flow of his logic to be challenged or questioned, there would be fewer weak arguments and poorly constructed sermons.[5]

If the minister had to face the opposition that a lawyer knows will meet his statements in court, he would soon become much more conservative in his assertions. When the minister in preaching says that "Darwin says thus-and-so" or "Ingersoll taught this-that-or-the-other," he would be greatly nonplused should some keen listener arise and ask him on what page of Darwin's works that statement may be found, or just where Ingersoll uttered the remark quoted. The minister who writes for publication learns this lesson—he cannot deal in generalities in writing as in speaking, for writing truly "maketh an exact man." But in speech the ordinary preacher is tempted to forget this and soar away in beautiful flights of oratory to heights where he overlooks the world—and some of the facts therein contained.

[5] Sermon published in the *Brooklyn Eagle,* April 18, 1927.

Hasty generalization is a serious fault anywhere, but nowhere is it more to be condemned, or more dangerous to the minister, than in a political fight. In preaching the ordinary sermon he can "get away" with sweeping assertions; but if he undertakes to tackle the evils of the city hall crowd with a few broad accusations or tell the county what he has heard about the "courthouse gang," he had better have in reserve his indictment of specific instances. Generalization will get him nowhere here. Let him be well informed beforehand that when he undertakes to fight long-entrenched political and social evil he engages in a conflict where no quarter is asked or given. After the first gasp of surprise that comes from the persons he attacks, he is going to find the ground beginning to shake beneath his feet. It is not a gentle maiden who is about to tap him lightly upon the wrist with her fan. They are out to "get that preacher" by fair means or foul. Ministers naturally shrink from warfare of this sort, but sometimes it must be undertaken. When it is, the righteous forces are often surprised and comforted to find what a power Truth can be to combat evil. Although the devil fights with fire, it is marvelous how Right seems to be its own self-evidencing witness, its own champion.

In summary, then, partisan or purely party questions should be left alone; but entering a civic or national fight on the side of a moral question is not only right but obligatory upon the minister, unless he, like Meroz, does not care to come out to the help of the Lord. One should be most certain that a moral issue is deeply involved, and to be certain of this should keep his eyes on the great righteous forces and tides of the people, not on the judgment of an isolated community. If the problem is complicated by local prejudices, personalities, old parties, ward bosses, etc., let the minister take all this into account. Then if, after all, he decides that it is his duty to "go in," let him, like Esther, put on his best apparel, theological, ecclesiastical, political, and personal, and approaching unto the most uncertain Ahasuerus of modern politics have as his motto, "If I perish, I perish." Thus recklessness and quick speaking shall be done away. But when all is said and done, it is a greater evil to stand idly by and see right worsted and wrong triumph than perchance to emerge at length from conflict with armor battered and dinted but "valiant for truth." For such a one, to paraphrase Bunyan, "all the trumpets will sound on the other side."

CHAPTER IV

Relations With Brother Ministers

Relations with professional brethren present problems in ethics and etiquette. In fact in such codes of ministerial ethics as have been developed, the nucleus has been the attempt to clarify the relationship between members of the profession. "Ministerial ethics" to most ministers means the way they feel they should treat their brother ministers; and, even more, the way they feel their brother ministers should treat them.

Henry Ward Beecher once asserted that it was not good for ministers to associate too much with each other nor to develop a "class consciousness." Another clergyman decried the way the professions, including the ministry, "flock together and see things in their own light." While this might indeed be dangerous if carried too far, yet the growth of a great conscious brotherhood is a magnificent thing, especially when this brotherhood is composed of men who are ministers of God. Why should not this brotherhood be able to make rules for its own members? If lawyers are the sole judges as to who may be disbarred from the practice of law, and if physicians have a code governing their relations with each other, why may not ministers recognize that they, too, have a brotherhood which may well look to each of them for conformity to its ideals? Ministers, of course, will not and should not yield upon that prin-

71

ciple which is at the heart of Protestantism—that every man must find in his own conscience his guide. A ministerial brotherhood able to prescribe and enforce rules upon all its members would destroy the very freedom in which each member of that brotherhood ought to stand. Nevertheless there is a suggestive value, a guiding value, in the attitudes and pronouncements of the ministerial brotherhood itself; and nowhere is this stronger than at those points where ministers measure and evaluate the propriety of their conduct toward each other.[1]

Duty to predecessor

Always there is a predecessor, and always his successor owes much to him. In a notable address "Ministerial Ethics" Bishop Charles B. Galloway said:

Much of our work is to reap where others have sown. Their sowing should have equal honor with our reaping. A circuit, station, or district may be served the full term without the earnest pastor's noting much fruit of his labor. Another comes whose mission is to gather the golden sheaves and whose joy it is to sing the harvest song. Though possibly much honored, credited with being a more successful workman, he really enjoys the fruit of another's planting. . . . The apostle Paul said: "Now he that planteth and watereth are one."[2]

Most ministers agree that the best plan of work when one first

[1] "As members of the same profession and brothers in the service of a common Master, the relation between ministers should be one of frankness and coöperation." (*Congregational Code,* III, 5. *Presbyterian Code* identical. The *Methodist Code* is identical except the last line, where it has, "of frankness, of comradeship, and of coöperation.")
"It is his duty to show a friendly and coöperative interest in his brethren, attending the group meetings of the ministers, assisting his brother ministers with labors of love, defending them against injustice, and following them with kindly concern in their hours of need or distress." (*Unitarian Code,* IV, 6.)
[2] Published in *Great Men and Great Movements.*

comes into a parish is to study the predecessor's methods and plans and continue them as best one can. In the beginning there should be no radical break with his methods. Indeed Bishop Galloway, in the address referred to above, made this injunction quite strong:

He [the minister] should endeavor to carry out his predecessor's well-formed plans . . . a wise master builder must leave many proposed works uncompleted. They require time for their full development. . . . Nothing is more common than for a pastor's cherished enterprises to lose or lapse when he moves to another field. His successor doubts their wisdom, considers others more important, and, with a self-conceit that would be ludicrous if the results were not serious, haughtily declares: "I have my own plans; another's I never could follow."

At any rate, local self-government and customs ought never to be harshly jarred upon a new man's arrival. The new minister needs all the popularity he can gather the first few weeks. It will do no good, but actual harm, to inaugurate at once sweeping changes in order to let the people know that a new hand is at the helm. In a few weeks, when conditions are better known, when the "well-formed" plans are known from the "ill-formed" which belonged to the former regime, the new pastor can then get into his own stride and guide his people into the best of everything.

It seems the part of modesty as well as of tact to refrain from telling a great deal of personal history, opinions, methods, etc., on one's first appearance in a new work. Let the people find out their pastor for themselves. Facts for the benefit of local papers may be given, of course, with photographs, but before the congregation it is best to take charge quietly and proceed to work. "Let not him that girdeth on his harness boast himself as he that putteth it off," would be an Old Testament proverb which will fit here. Furthermore, there are always the curious who are out to look the new man over on his first appearance, and who, when they know all about him, will lapse into their usual state of religious desuetude. It will not hurt to keep this crowd guessing—and coming—a little longer, before they resume their natural positions.

Every pastor will find, on entering a new parish, that he must deal with his *predecessor's special friends*. There are some people in every pastorate who will never feel toward a present pastor as kindly as they do to a certain former one. They hold him in memory as the best minister their church ever had. They will speak of his excellencies to each succeeding pastor and sigh with regret at his passing from their midst. They may be polite enough to add as an afterthought that of course they like their present pastor also—but that same present pastor well knows that he will never take the beloved predecessor's place in the hearts of certain individuals. It is well to be very kindly and sympathetic with these, and to remember the lover's advice and "praise a rival." Never for one moment should a minister permit himself to be irked by the ceaseless praise of a former pastor as it is dinned in his ears by devoted friends. If it is done purposely to worry one, as in some cases, it is answered best by appearing not to notice it; if it is done naturally, it should be just as naturally entered into. "Depreciation of a predecessor's efficiency ought to be as rare as it is reprehensible," said Galloway.

A minister is sometimes fretted by the tactless persons who delight to inform him that Brother Jones, the former pastor, never did as he is doing. One is powerfully tempted to tell these officious persons that they should behold and see that the present pastor is not now Brother Jones. The new schoolteacher can thus deal with a roomful of pupils, but the preacher should not. "Men have different plans," or "We are going to try this and see how it works"—such replies will usually assure good will at least from these persons.

Every minister discovers some persons who dislike the former pastor. As Galloway says:

Every man of positive convictions will have had some antagonisms. His style was not according to every taste. Some oversensitive ones felt themselves slighted. On his first pastoral round a preacher will discover that his predecessor had a blade that cut and a twanging bow that sent an arrow to the mark. He will hear criticisms favorable and unfavorable. Then and there he has an opportunity to display the true chivalrous brotherhood of the ministry. . . . He should remember . . . the very persons who discuss so freely his predecessor will give him a similar introduction to his successor.

This is true. It may be the part of wisdom to take advantage of any revived interest people may show when the new pastor appears, but under no circumstances should he let them hear a single word to the discredit of his predecessor. A criticism of a former minister given to persons of this type will go much further than if told to others. They will be glad to pass it on as ministerial approval of their lukewarmness or antipathy.[3]

---

[3] "It is unethical for a minister to speak ill of the character or work of another minister, especially of his predecessor or successor. It is the duty of a minister, however, in flagrant cases of unethical conduct, to bring the matter before the proper body." (*Congregational Code*, III, 4. *Presbyterian* and *Methodist Codes* identical.)

"I will refrain from speaking disparagingly about the work of either my predecessor or my successor." (*Disciples Code*, III.)

"He should always speak with good will of another minister, especially of the minister who has preceded or followed him in a parish. It may be his duty, however, to bring to the attention of the responsible officials of the fellowship any instance of gross professional or personal misconduct that may injure the good name of the ministry." (*Unitarian Code*, IV, 4.)

When a *former pastor* returns for a visit to his erstwhile parish, it is of course the duty of the incumbent minister to call upon him at the earliest opportunity as a mark of courtesy. If he has returned to perform a marriage ceremony or conduct a funeral, the local pastor will of course take the charitable position that the visitor was invited to come for such a duty and could scarcely refuse. Former pastors often feel that they must return when invited for such occasions, and the local man should understand that no intrusion is intended.[4]

If the contingency arises in which the visits of a predecessor are not casual or disinterested, trouble may be made. There is nothing that worries a minister more than for a former pastor to meddle with the affairs of his pastorate. This is a breach of etiquette on the part of the predecessor, of course, and will be dealt with later, but from the point of view of the local pastor what is the proper course to take? The best method is to attempt to find out what motive actuates the interfering brother. If it is earnest though ill-considered interest, it will not be hard to show him that his letters or his visits are not best for the work. If it is a natural desire or inclination to meddle and if all hints fail, then it may be necessary for the pastor to be perfectly frank with the interferer and let him know in plain words that he is no longer in charge, and that his visits are not welcomed.

Duty to a successor

When a new minister comes to a parish taking up duties and obligations with which he is not at all familiar, he instinctively turns to the man who can advise and help him more than any other—the outgoing pastor. He realizes that the new field holds the usual problems having to do with the interrelation of per-

---

[4] "I will be courteous to any predecessor of mine when he returns to the field, and will be thoughtful of any retired minister." (*Disciples Code*, III.)

sonalities; the usual civic and public questions; the usual plans, half-done, all-done, or un-done. The outgoing minister is familiar with all such and furthermore knows of many hidden though important matters that the incoming man should be aware of. The rocks that line the ministerial channel are known to him, but not to his successor. The unanimous voice of ministers everywhere therefore asserts that it is a prime duty of every outgoing pastor to meet with and advise the new man of local conditions.

He should be ready to give a broad survey of the field and its work. If time permits, details may be discussed. If it is possible to go over the entire roll of the church together, the incoming man will thus be able to gain an insight into conditions, which will be of inestimable service to him. Every minister feels himself obligated to supply all this and other helpful information to his successor, but at the same time he should be on guard lest he seem to be directing future work. One may well advise and state methods previously followed, but the minister of tact will know how to make it clear that the situation is now entirely in the hands of the new man.[5]

Some of the older men of the ministry have remarked that it is not wise for the outgoing minister to tell the new man everything he may know concerning the people of the church. If there are hidden rocks in the channel, the new pilot should be apprised of them; but there are dark, unfathomed caves in the pastoral deep, which, discovered accidentally by one pastor, need never be known to another. What a new minister does not know does not always hurt him. Let every man find out some things for himself. A new pastor's ignorance will give him a good

---

[5] "The minister should be very generous in responding to reasonable requests for assistance from his brother minister and his denominational officials, remembering that he is one of a larger fellowship." (*Unitarian Code*, IV, 5.)

start toward solving many problems. He will be able blissfully and ignorantly to drive a coach and four through many a tangled knot composed of unregenerate personalities and general "cussedness" simply because he does not know what his predecessor knows, and everybody knows he doesn't know. The new preacher should be told much, but not everything. Give the people a chance as well as the preacher.

Every minister should give his successor a good "send-off" with the people. To quote Galloway again:

The character of the introduction and commendation which he gives will determine the welcome his successor receives and will have a potent influence upon the entire history of his pastorate. If doubts are expressed as to his ability or availability, if fears are intimated that he lacks at certain vital points or has some objectionable peculiarities, if confidential predictions of failure are made "just to one or two very special and discreet friends," the brother comes with a mountain of prejudice to scale and silent but positive opposition to conquer. On the contrary, if he commends his virtues, applauds his abilities, tells of his fidelities, rejoices in his successes, and congratulates his old flock that they are to be under such competent and consecrated pastoral care, he comes with hearts to welcome him, spiritual sympathy to sustain him, and assured victory to cheer him.

Even when a retiring minister finds himself in the position of a discredited or rejected man, he should be Christianly disposed toward his successor. Just as every child deserves the right to be wellborn, so every minister deserves the right to a good start in any new field he may enter.

It is usually conceded that in general it is better for a retiring minister to leave both church and parish before the new man comes to take charge. A former pastor's presence should not be allowed to serve as the nucleus for the crystallizing regret of his many friends. It is also best for the outgoing man to dodge the opening reception if there be one. The king is dead—let him stay dead (or out of sight). Long live the king!

Church property, church records, especially the house which is to be occupied by the new minister, should all be turned over to him in good condition.[6] This he has a right to expect. Lloyd C. Douglas gave minute directions in *The Minister's Everyday Life* as to just how thoroughly the parsonage must be cleaned for the new man—first with the broom, then with a mop, and then over everything again with a silk handkerchief!

Above all, when a man leaves a charge, let him leave it. No minister should be constantly going back to gossip with the brethren or hear comments on the work of his successor. Great harm has been done in this way by some ministers. The outgoing pastor should get all his supplies—trunks, boxes, barrels, the piano, the typewriter, the breadbox, the garden hose, and Willie's shotgun—loaded at one time, should give all a good-by, making it as tearful as desired, but having started the moving van, look not back! Although his successor may not admit it, the presence of the former pastor after that will be embarrassing to the new man. "Get out and stay out" is the injunction here.

The difficult question may arise as to how to proceed when an old parishioner, or an especially friendly family, may ask a former pastor to return and officiate at the wedding of a daughter of the house, or to conduct the funeral of some loved one. Such matters can usually be arranged best through the local pastor, if the family involved will take him into their confidence. He

[6] "It is unethical for a minister on leaving a charge to leave the parsonage property in other than first-class condition, with all dirt, rubbish, etc., removed. Common courtesy to his successor demands the observance of the golden rule." (*Methodist Code.*)

will be glad to transmit the invitation to the desired minister and the latter in turn to respond. Unless the local pastor is an extremely touchy and jealous individual, he will be agreeable to any wishes the family may have; if not, let his confusion be upon his own head. At any rate the parishioners should proceed through their own pastor. If he does not actually transmit the invitation, he should be aware of it. This is a courtesy due him, and the invited minister must know it if the people do not.

Sometimes the people do not understand this matter as well as do ministers. Perhaps they shrink from informing their present pastor that they prefer another minister to perform a daughter's marriage ceremony. He "might be hurt" if he is not asked to officiate. Perhaps they do not like their pastor and do not see how it is any of his business whom they ask. So they go over the head of the local man and ask a ministerial service from their beloved former pastor—and this puts the beloved former pastor in an embarrassing position. He cannot accept without offending his brother minister; he cannot decline without offending the family or friend.

Under these circumstances ministers of experience have stated that they write a tactful communication to the persons who thus request their services, expressing pleasure at the invitation, but mentioning that as a matter of form it would be well to consult the local pastor; that he no doubt will be agreeable to their plans, but as a courtesy that ministers usually pay one another this is due him. It may be tactfully added also that the present pastor should be given some part in the ceremony if possible.

Such a message generally gets the right results. When the actual occasion is at hand, if no provision has been made to recognize the local minister in the ceremonies, the minister in charge need feel no hesitancy in suggesting it. Thus all brotherliness shall be fulfilled.[7]

Galloway felt that it was "positively reprehensible for an ex-pastor to take advantage of his personal attachments to secure the honor of officiating at marriages in his former charges." This may be admitted if the ex-pastor be the instigator of an invitation in a conscious way, but where it comes to him unasked and unsought he may be excused. His procedure in such a case has been outlined. Galloway also felt it wrong to hold on to a former pastorate through correspondence: "I would also advise against confidential and voluminous correspondence with old parishioners. It invites petty criticism and encourages reliance upon other counsel and leadership."

In spite of all this, it ought to be said that the breaking of the pastoral tie is no light matter. Often the minister and his family make friends and form connections which transcend the pastoral tie and which only death may dissolve. For such friends the home of the minister is always open and to these he pours out his soul. For them he discards the outward wrappings which surround his calling and shows them himself. And to the mutual glory of the minister and his friends be it said that more often than not these persons who know the minister best as a man follow him closest as a servant of God. It would give much pain and add nothing special to the glory of the church were such ties to be severed when the minister moves. If he is tactful, he will know how to continue as friend and yet cease to be pastor.

---

[7] "I will refrain from frequent visits to a former field and if, in exceptional cases, I am called back for a funeral or a wedding, I will request that the resident minister be invited to participate in the service." (*Disciples Code*, III.)

Invitations to other churches

When a minister is invited by a group or society of another church to bring some message upon a public occasion, or perhaps to occupy the pulpit in the absence of the pastor, he should always make sure that the invitation is known and approved by the preacher in charge. Some church organizations take it upon themselves to form their own programs without respect to the minister of the church. This may never bring any complications; but when an outside minister receives an invitation from such an organization, he ought, before accepting, to make sure that the minister of the church to be visited is informed of his coming. The pastor in charge may wish to be present on the occasion in question and officially welcome the visitor, as he should if convenient. A pastor might be very properly indignant should he find that another minister has been in his church or parish in an official and representative way and he himself was not aware of it. He might be blamed by some for not being present to welcome the guest of the occasion. So in all cases such invitations had better be "developed" somewhat before accepting them, and the suggestion tactfully advanced that the local pastor ought to know and signify approval before an outsider can wholeheartedly accept.[8]

---

[8] "It is unethical for a minister to interfere directly or indirectly with the parish work of another minister." (*Congregational Code*, III, 1. *Presbyterian* and *Methodist Codes* identical.)

"Ministerial service should not be rendered to the members of another parish without consulting the minister of the parish, or by invitation from him." (*Methodist Code.*)

"Ministerial service should not be rendered to the members of another parish without consulting the minister of that parish." (*Congregational Code*, III, 2.)

"It is unethical for a minister to render professional service within the parish of another minister, or occupy another minister's pulpit, without the consent of that minister, whenever obtainable, and this consent should be given readily." (*Unitarian Code*, IV, 1.)

An exception may be made in those cases where, through long-continued association and co-operation, neighboring pastors are so sure of each other and each other's people that when one is invited to the other's church he takes it for granted that his presence there will be welcomed by the minister in charge.

There is an ethical procedure which ought to be followed by an outside minister in the matter of supplying another's pulpit even when that is legally controlled by the congregation or some committee. When there is perfect good will between pastor and pulpit-supply committee, this matter never becomes acute, and when the pastor is absent, for instance, he is glad to have his pulpit supplied by whomever his people choose. But in case a minister is invited whose disagreement with the pastor is known to all, his presence can be construed in no other way than as a reflection upon the pastor of the church. If the people object to their pastor, let them get rid of him in a constitutional manner; until they do, he *is* their pastor and must be treated as such.

New and visiting ministers

When a person moves into a new community immemorial custom demands that the first visit should be made by the local people. This is a courtesy that every pastor should remember with regard to "new ministers" who move in to take over the pastorate of a sister denomination, or any visiting minister whose presence touches the life of the local people. Such visitors and new pastors have the right to expect this courtesy from the local ministry.

Inquiry, however, among our present-day ministers makes evident the fact that this brotherly amenity is not observed with any regularity. Asked the direct question as to whether on their arrival at their new parishes they were called upon by the local ministers and their wives, such ministers replied almost unanimously, "Very seldom." Pastors indeed are busy, but should not be too preoccupied with their own work to greet a brother hospitably as he begins his.

When a minister is a visitor in a community the local clergy have the pleasant duty of extending him the courtesies which belong to visitors the world over. Lavish entertainment is neither expected nor desired by clergymen when they are visiting, especially if they are on a regular preaching mission; but the fellowship of a modest meal together or the welcome calls of brother ministers have often proved a mutual blessing as well as the fulfilling of the old law of hospitality. The great denominations at their conventions and conferences usually create a "committee on courtesies" in order to welcome visitors and look after kindred amenities.

Duty to ministers of other denominations

Fortunately interchurch rivalry has died down with the passing years, and the stern denominationalism of an earlier age has all but disappeared. Nevertheless between local churches, especially in small towns, there is considerable counting of noses, comparing of local efforts, and striving for local prestige. "In a Competitive Pulpit" was the succinct title of an article by Walter Dudley Cavert which appeared in the religious press some years ago. This article pointed out and deprecated the fact that often ministers are in competition with each other rather than with the evil they all should fight.

He [the minister] is hired to produce visible tangible results for his particular congregation and often he cannot strengthen his own organization without detracting from the possibilities of the sister church across the road. . . . The minister is in a position hardly different from that of the business man who finds it impossible to increase his own trade without taking customers away from his rival on the opposite corner. He is always under the temptation of thinking in terms of his own personal advantage.[9]

Unlovely rivalry and professional jealousy are indeed abominable, but there is sometimes a healthy provoking of one another to good works. The "one-church" town, like the proverbial "one-horse" town, is rather a spiritless proposition. Consolidation of church forces where possible and co-operation at all times are principles always to be followed, but in actual fact there is usually a field wide enough for all. The harvest of the unchurched is as plenteous as ever. Every Christian minister has a right to reach out and gather all he can for his Master without interfering in any way with the garnering done by his brother.

Proselyting the members of other churches is universally condemned by ministers of all denominations. As Galloway put it: "Our field is the world and not some other church; and our mission is to feed, not steal, sheep." This is absolute.[10]

Occasionally, however, a member of one church seeks of his own volition to join another. He may have married a member of the church he desires to join; he may feel more at home there; he may have taken a dislike to his own pastor and wishes to injure him seriously by leaving his pastoral care. At any rate he comes and asked to be allowed to join the other fellowship. What about it?

In all cases of this sort it is the part of manliness as well as of

[9] *Christian Century*, July 12, 1939.

[10] "Especially should he be careful to avoid the charge of proselyting." (*Congregational Code*, III, 1. *Methodist* and *Presbyterian Codes* practically identical.)

"He should be very careful not to proselytize among the members of another church." (*Unitarian Code*, IV, 2.)

courtesy for the pastor to whom the applicant comes to confer with the pastor who is to be left. If the facts are clear the other minister can be trusted to release the member, and if denominational law permits perhaps give him a certificate of transfer. At any rate it is not ethical to receive a member of another church without informing his previous pastor of the action contemplated, and the best results are secured by a personal interview between pastors.

Ministers usually feel free to receive members of other churches when these come of their own accord after they have followed the procedure outlined above. But as Galloway said:

Sacred Church ties ought not to be severed except for the most solemn considerations of duty. And the only office of the pastor whose communion is sought is to instruct the inquirer, but never to unsettle faith nor encourage the coming. In my own pastoral experience I have in several instances advised the applicant to remain in his old Church home.

Ministers will do well to learn just why the new member wishes to come in. "Spite members," like spite marriages, do not last. The fact that a man was "hurt" by a former pastor is not an especially good reason for accepting his membership.

There are homes in every community that are "spheres of influence" of certain churches. The entire home circle may not be members of the church in question, but from tradition or inclination the family is counted as belonging to a certain denomination. Ministers of other churches should respect such denominational ties. Unchurched homes are, of course, fair campaigning ground for all; but where the nominal allegiance of a family is to one church this should be remembered by the workers of other denominations.

Every minister will at times have occasion to visit in the

homes of the members of other denominations—sometimes social calls, sometimes business, sometimes sympathetic, as, for instance, after a death. Most ministers stumble into the wrong homes at times, and in small places each minister is often thrown in contact with the members of other churches. In all this, however, the earnest, straightforward minister never offends nor attempts to usurp a rightful pastor's place. His brother ministers have him sized up after a brief observation of his work. Their measure is not made by the letter of the law, but by the spirit of it. They allow him a great many liberties with their people when he earns their confidence, but if he is a "sheep stealer" the gates of brotherhood are soon barred against him.

In small places *local conflicts* sometimes occur between denominations and churches in such things as times for special programs, meetings, etc. Many of these conflicts may be eliminated by a local ministers' conference or by mutual acquaintance with the program of every other church. In small places an unusual or well-advertised program at one church becomes a town affair and draws from the other churches. Each congregation is, of course, anxious to keep its own crowd, and the minister is human enough to feel that he must at least hold his own. Thus rivalry may arise in securing speakers and celebrities, and once this starts it goes a long way before it stops. Fortunately the great mass of preachers co-operate in local work and avoid anything which would cause jealousy. Where a conflict in special programs occurs, an explanation is usually given by the one responsible. So much for interdenominational law which, like international law, must enforce itself by the sanction of public opinion.

It ought to be said, however, that one minister whose zeal and enthusiasm are greater than his judgment can upset a whole ring of local churches. If he and his church, his picture, and his opinions are in every paper, while the bandwagon crowd follows him and the town tells what a live wire he is, it may stir the ecclesiastical dust and cobwebs out of the other churches, but we have seen it stir a good many other things also—including a sullen hostility. There are greater things than publicity and energy in the world. The good opinion of other ministers is worth more in the long run than the plaudits of the crowd. Reality, at any rate, has a strange way of manifesting itself; and when a man is found to be genuine, whatever be his methods, his brethren neither fear him nor are jealous of him—they rejoice with him, for he is one of them.

CHAPTER V

The Pastoral Ministry

"He gave some to be . . . pastors." The apostle, the prophet, and the evangelist may outrank the pastor ecclesiastically, but the triumph remains in the hands of the man who goes in and out among his people, visiting the sick, binding up the broken-hearted, living the Life. So it has come to be observed in our own era, as in the long history of the Christian Church, that the pastor is able to take the control of things out of the hands of either prophet or evangelist if ever there be need—as there never should be. The grade of a man as pastor will make up most of the ministerial average when final records are in. "Two-thirds pastoral ability and one-third preaching" was an old-fashioned measure of ministerial ability. That, however, was before the day of the social engineering and executive work that now count so heavily in that final average. At any rate to be a successful minister of God a man must be primarily a pastor, and this should be both known and understood.

Pastoral calling

A wise and experienced older clergyman once observed that next to knowing how to conduct the sacred offices of the church, the young ministers with whom he has talked have always wished to know how properly to make a pastoral call. Calling upon people of diverse occupations, sexes, states of health, manner of life, etc., is a difficult task, and ministers have a tendency to shrink from the labor involved in it. It is not so much the time or physical effort required, but the tension, the constant outpouring of nervous energy, the studied effort to size up the situation in every home and treat it accordingly—all this is wearing on the men of the ministry.

To a certain extent the old-fashioned type of pastoral call has been discarded. City pastorates are often large; rural parishioners are scattered; and it is manifestly impossible in some situations for one pastor to cover the entire membership. Were pastoral work and preaching the only obligations resting upon a minister he might very well give himself completely to these two duties. But the multiplicity of other tasks falling upon him has cut heavily into the time he might otherwise give to visiting. Some of these responsibilities—committee work, group meetings, public and representative events—while they take needed time, may have a value in helping the minister to work at first hand with his people and so tie tighter the pastoral bond. But it is well for the pastor to remember that his presence in an individual's home brings him in far more intimate contact with the people who live there than any amount of letter writing or committee work can do. As has been aptly said: "The world does not want *things;* it wants *persons.*"

Asked the direct question as to whether they think pastoral calling is as important, less important, or more important than it used to be, half of the ministerial authorities questioned affirm that it is just as important as ever, while a third regard it as even more important. "The increasing impersonalizing of urban life" is given by one distinguished pastor as his reason for holding this latter view. But irrespective of any difference of opinion on

90

this matter all ministers unite in agreeing that pastoral calling ought to be done as much as is humanly possible.

The universal regret of modern ministers is that they cannot find time to do this part of their work thoroughly. A number of them, however, claim that they manage to visit all the homes of their people systematically and regularly. One energetic Baptist minister writes that he gets into every home in his church—and he has over two thousand members—once every year; and that this accomplishment requires "two afternoons a week for thirty-six weeks, three hours an afternoon." His calls are necessarily short, about ten minutes each, but he gets them made.

Practically all other pastors state that they hold general systematic visitation as an ideal, but that emergencies in the membership, sick calls, and visits to new people consume most of the time they can allot to calling. The size of the congregation is a determining factor. When a church is so large that no one man can carry on this phase of his work without constantly neglecting other important duties, some other procedure must be followed. Those members who have problems or who need special pastoral help are encouraged to seek the pastor in his office, while an assistant pastor is often employed by large churches to share some of the work of visiting. Priority in all pastoral calling is, of course, given to the sick and bereaved, with visits of welcome to new people taking second place. The aged and shut-ins are also on the preferred list. For the rest, the busy minister does all that he can and when he wearily sinks into his bed at night quite often remembers with chagrin another needed call which he failed to make. A good shepherd literally does give his life for the sheep.

Concerning the visits of an assistant pastor, or of professional lay workers, or of visiting committees from the membership, it should be said that these often prove of great help. They cement the church together, make people feel that the church cares for them, and usually bring a blessing on their own account. But it should never be forgotten that the people do not consider that such visits are visits from their pastor. With Protestant people no one minister ever takes the place of another. They like the assistant for *himself* and the pastor for *himself*, and in great trouble they want their pastor to hurry to them. Every minister should be aware of this desire of his people.

On the credit side it should be remembered that pastoral visiting, in addition to its value to people and church, is vastly helpful to the pastor himself. Going in and out of the homes of his people takes time that might be given to reading and study, but it opens before him a very real book of life. By some indirect but powerful alchemy the things a minister learns in visiting his people—conversational chitchat, personal aspirations, trivial home happenings—become transmuted into sermonic material that can bless and help. Something is always added to a man's preaching when his pastoral visiting is steady and regular, and something vital goes from it when he ceases to visit. A housegoing preacher not only makes a churchgoing people, but the man himself is enabled to gear his messages to his people's needs.

The minister is cautioned by all to avoid showing *partiality* to any special group, class, or faction among his members, nor should his visiting be confined to any definite group or district. This needs but to be mentioned to be approved. The good pastor, like the good parent or teacher, has no favorites. He has, of course, his own special friends and congenial spirits, and he would be something else than human were this not so, but officially he is careful to hold all his people as equal and serve them equally. Certain persons, of course, need his attention more than others, but these—the sick, the dying, the aged—are from every social class and from every part of his parish. The usual pastor finds, too, that some persons in his church need more pastoral attention than others, and like the Good Shepherd he often leaves the ninety and nine and goes out after the one who otherwise might be lost. This is understood. But to get the reputation of being a minister to the rich alone, or to outcasts alone, or to intellectuals alone, or to any one special group, is not good.[1]

Apropos of partiality, a pastor should avoid making a difference in the way he greets people at the door of his church, or when visitors, friends, or new people are passing by him. He should not show greater pleasure at meeting one than another, but sometimes he obviously dismisses one with detached impersonality only to greet the next with warmth and enthusiasm. People are much more sensitive at this point than is sometimes realized. One of the best-loved pastors of today, who enjoys a national reputation, has the happy faculty of making each person he greets feel that he is supremely important. No minister can be perfunctory with persons—the couple being married is at that moment the all-important couple, the new member being received into the church the all-important member.

[1] "It is unethical for a minister to take sides with factions in his parish." (*Congregational Code*, II, 5. *Presbyterian Code* similar.)

"In my administrative and pastoral duties I will be impartial so no one can truthfully say that I am pastor of only one group in the church." (*Disciples Code*, II.)

"The minister should remember that he is pastor of all his people. He should avoid the display of preferences and the cultivation of intimacies within the parish which may be construed as evidence of partiality. He should not attach himself to any social set either in the church or in the community. He should not allow personal feelings to interfere with the impartial nature of his ministrations." (*Unitarian Code*, III, 1.)

"In the case of parish controversy, the minister should maintain an attitude of good will to all, even when he himself is the subject of the controversy." (*Unitarian Code*, III, 2.)

Should a pastor make a *professional* or a *social* call? Ministers revolt at the implications of either of these words. "Professional" in the sense of something perfunctory or stereotyped is an abomination to sincere ministers. A visit that gives the impression that since it is a minister's business to talk this way therefore this is the way he talks is worse than useless. "A pastoral call should not be made at all unless made well," Bernard Clausen said in *The Technique of a Minister*. On the other hand a social call, one that seemingly disavows the deeper reasons for pastoral calling, that skims lightly over anything but an affable camaraderie, means very little. A good minister will wonder whether he might not have cultivated friendly relations with a particular home in some other way than by spending precious minutes in friendly chitchat. To be sure a certain amount of easy conversation and the observance of social amenities is expected of the minister as of any other person, and especially in getting acquainted with new people one moves slowly until a rapport is achieved. Also, in homes where he is well known and loved, the ease of assured friendship gives an opportunity for converse on all sorts of matters of interest. But present-day ministers feel that the pastoral call should be made to count for something more than the mere cultivation of friendly relations and that it can be of tremendous value.

Quite a few approve the old principle which Washington Gladden laid down in *The Christian Pastor and the Working Church*—that the pastoral call should be social but religious conversation should not be avoided. Others, however, are more decisive and definitely steer the conversation into channels of Christian thought. Still others go much further; they definitely take over as the spiritual adviser of the home and make the moments count toward a definite end. When this is done sincerely by a pastor who loves his people and is loved in turn, the finest sort of ministerial work may be accomplished. "I do not get to this home often," one good pastor is accustomed to say. "I may not be back for a long time. I have many others to look after. But while I am here I want to make the minutes count toward getting you and your family closer to God. Let's talk about it." What home could resist a sincere appeal like that, or fail to respond with an equal sincerity?

"Every call is different," a prominent minister of central Indiana correctly states, and situations govern procedures in each instance. It seems, however, that since pastoral calling is a part of the minister's work he need be under no more fear of becoming professional when making a call than when he is preaching a sermon. When he comes into a home he is welcomed as pastor, nor may he divest himself of that character with anything like ease. Everything, therefore, is in favor of his acting naturally as the spiritual adviser and guide to the home, and he ought to measure up to the privilege.

Should the pastor have *prayer* with each call? It depends. A few ministers state that their invariable rule is to have prayer regardless of circumstances, but the majority report that they leave this to the moment itself. Prayer, however, even with a single individual and in the midst of daily life, has a spiritual value all its own.

Murray II. Leiffer's study of lay attitudes toward the minister and his duties brought out the fact that laymen wish their minister to "feel free to pray" during a pastoral visit if occasion warrants, but that parishioners "dread the arrival of the unimaginative pastor who believes it necessary to kneel and offer a lengthy prayer at the conclusion of each call." However, the study reveals that when asked the definite question, "How acceptable will a minister be in your church if he seldom prays during pastoral calls?" all groups responded unfavorably.[2]

It would seem, therefore, that the minister should enter a home with the idea that he will have a brief, helpful prayer before he leaves *unless* conditions make praying inappropriate, rather than with the negative attitude that he may perhaps have prayer *if* conditions demand it.

It would be impossible to outline or describe the different situations in which a minister finds himself as a pastor paying a call. One general rule might, however, be suggested as a guide in this difficult matter: it should be the aim of the pastor to make himself a part of the home while he calls, but at the same time to guard his own essential character.

That is to say, adaptation to each home and its atmosphere will give a man at once an open path to the hearts of his people. To feel that they "have known him always" is a high compliment which some ministers are able to wrest from a family upon their first call. This means that they have instantly sensed and sized up the home and its inmates and come in as one of them. At the same time the last part of the rule above cannot be too strongly insisted upon. The minister must not forego his own characteristics nor minimize the essential nature of his calling. Because poor grammar is used or because dirt is in evidence he need not break the king's English nor wear dirty linen upon his person—far otherwise. He must be himself and not let go one jot or tittle of the things which make him what he is.

To put this in other words, there should be an ease of manner and approach to the most pretentious as well as to the simplest home. This ease of bearing begets a confidence and a trust almost at once. There is no one who arouses more uncertainty and

[2] *The Layman Looks at the Minister.*

uneasiness in us than the one who is himself uneasy. A pastor who is uncertain of himself and his mission and his reception in any home, or who by an apologetic air or a hat-in-hand attitude comes nervously into a strange house will make mutual understanding very difficult. Simplicity in all situations is a great desideratum. If one is in earnest, this is not hard to achieve. If the visiting pastor wishes to be a helpful friend to a poor family among his people, the members of that family will sense his wish and will believe in him. If he goes under the turrets of the rich with the idea that he has something for them which no one else may bring, they too will believe—these people who by their very wealth are isolated from so much of life.[3]

The other side of this rule should now be remembered. In neither the hovel of the poor nor the palace of the rich should the pastor lose his distinctive identity in order to secure an "approach." "Adaptation without losing essential character" is the rule. If anything must be broken, it must be the adaptation. Better be unable to visit a home, better be unwelcome or disliked in a home, than to forswear ministerial characteristics and be ignored as a spiritual representative. Pastoral visiting ends when a man is not a pastor.

Office calls

Of late years, especially in large pastorates and in cities, office calls have come to play a definite part in ministerial life. It is possible to take care of a certain amount of pastoral work in such a way; indeed some ministers frankly encourage their people to come to see them, rather than vice versa. Ministers have always been open to approach by their people; but with the rise of pastoral counseling and the difficulty of obtaining privacy

[3] "In my pastoral calling, I will have respect for every home I enter for I am a representative of Christ and the Church." (*Disciples Code,* II.)

in home interviews, ministers have evolved a system of office appointments similar to those of a doctor.

An office at the church rather than the minister's own intimate study is quite often set as the place where such pastoral counseling may be given, but of course there must be absolute privacy in all such interviews. Persons in need of their pastor's advice and comfort often shrink from having it known that they are seeking him. Sometimes they hesitate to make an appointment through the church secretary, preferring to approach the minister himself. However, in large cities a certain impersonality and anonymity are taken for granted, and where regular and well-known office hours are kept by a pastor most people will go to see him when they feel the need. But sensitive persons, often the very ones who need help most, hesitate to come openly to the church office. Then the minister must arrange a convenient time and place to see them.

A famous clergyman-psychiatrist of Baltimore in addressing a group of ministers upon this matter stated that he had found it a good plan to be in a certain pew of his church at definite hours; in this fashion he made it easy for those too timid to seek him otherwise. Karl Ruf Stolz suggested a stroll through the woods or park as an opportune way for pastor and member to talk, especially if the member is responsive to the appeal of nature. Dean Stolz also emphasized the value of putting the consultant at ease and, if the interview is in the study, giving him a seat not directly in front of the pastor but at his side, and perhaps in "faint shadows rather than in the bright light."

Sympathy and understanding are the qualities most called for, and very often the minister finds that in listening he does his best service. Two situations requiring caution should be mentioned: when the visiting party is totally unknown or of an uncertain or enigmatic character—certain types of neurotic women, for instance—it is well for the minister to have his wife, secretary, or a friend somewhere within call; when it is evident that mental derangement is involved, the pastor must be on guard more than ever.

It cannot be stressed too often that pastoral interviews and everything relating to them are to be kept absolutely secret by the minister. Any reference to such interviews—alluding publicly to what "one who visited me recently" said; or, "a man came to see me once and told this story"—may illustrate a point but will set the congregation to wondering of whom their pastor is speaking, and will make them fearful of confiding in him. Some very excellent counselors have been remiss here and, thinking that they might disguise names and persons, have repeated confidences entrusted to them under the ministerial confessional.

A distinguished Episcopal clergyman, the rector of one of the famous churches of New York, enjoys a reputation as a great pastor. A publisher once asked him to put into a book some of the remarkable pastoral experiences and life situations in which he has figured—stories which would be widely read and greatly appreciated—urging that fictitious names and disguised allusions would maintain privacy. "No," said the rector with firmness, "it cannot be done. No matter how I tried to disguise, there are some who would know. I received those stories in confidence and they will die with me."

Ministers should at all times be careful in the matter of *light comment and idle gossip*, especially regarding persons and matters of local interest. But nowhere should one watch his words more carefully than while making a series of pastoral calls. Words thoughtlessly spoken are often remembered and given surprising interpretations after the minister has gone. It should be remembered, too, that many people read little and think less; and if their own snap judgments or prejudiced comment is thoughtlessly approved by the minister while he calls, they may be able to quote him as their authority in all future references. Another class, especially in smaller cities and towns, usually finds its chief interest in local personalities and neighborhood matters. Ministers of the better sort avoid any semblance of carrying details of family or neighborhood gossip.

Successful pastors also warn their brethren against speaking in a disparaging way of anyone in the local church unless done for a worthy motive and in a very guarded way. Unless it is necessary it should never be done, for promiscuous comment on church personalities is deadly. The way Mrs. Smith holds her head when she sings in church may be perfectly ridiculous, but the wise minister knows better than to make a remark to that effect. The pastor may know some very amusing stories about the Joneses; but should he forget some evening in the Smith family circle and "take off" old Brother Jones's peculiar mannerisms, he may hear from it later. The story was so good, the imitation so perfect, that the Smiths pass it on with due credit for authorship (it ought to be handsomely illustrated with a woodcut of the author—a square, solid block of wood, cut) and then the Jones connection gets hold of it and there is a great withdrawal and coolness among the Joneses. "Unless he enjoins a fine restraint upon this indulgence of his delightful gift [humor], he may live to recall, with humiliating self-abasement, the occasions when he had played the buffoon and clown," as Lloyd C. Douglas commented in *The Minister's Everyday Life.*

Relationships with women

Women make up a large proportion of the minister's flock, and the pastoral relationship with them is complicated by the fact that they *are* women. For a long time there was a natural shrinking on the part of ecclesiastical writers from discussing matters that pertain to sex in connection with church work; but we live in a day when we are anxious to see things just as they are, and when, furthermore, we have been enlightened several times by front-page headlines announcing to the world that another minister has stumbled.

Ministers must visit women quite often in a pastoral capacity. The man who thinks he can get out of this is much mistaken. He will find young women and old women among his membership—sick and well, rich and poor, great and small. Even if he confines his visits to the sick alone, he will find that a large proportion of these will be women. This fact had better be understood beforehand by himself, his wife, and his people.

In an article on this subject, Henry H. Barstow said that it is a tactical error for a minister to devote too much of his ministry to women. "Men and young people sense it and make their own comments. He will never reach uninterested men and boys by specializing on the women." [4] However, we should say that whatever member needs the pastor should receive his attention, regardless of sex or any other condition. Most ministers would much prefer to work with men, but this may not always be done. The ideal minister will hold all his people equal in his heart. There is neither male nor female, bond nor free, Greek nor barbarian in the kingdom of which he is made a minister.

The danger in ministerial service to women is not so much error on the minister's part—though there are doubtless silly women in church as well as out, and there are weak brethren—but the causing of comment and gossip which would embarrass the minister's service. The merest nothing will start a scandal, and the sensible minister knows it and acts accordingly.

Henry Wilder Foote advised that calls alone upon young

[4] "The Minister and Women," *Church Management*, November, 1926.

married women in the absence of the husband should be avoided. He also suggested that some other person should be taken along, and this is a sensible procedure when calling upon a woman whose character is known to be doubtful. Repeated calls upon any one woman should be avoided, since these will give rise to talk. Anything that will cause gossip should be shunned.

When a woman is sick and in bed the minister should always be sure that someone else is with her when he calls. It is a good rule to find out beforehand if she cares to see him. Wise pastors usually try to have the nurse or attendant go before to arrange the room for the visit.

When a minister comes to be well known in a community he need not be so vigilantly on guard against gossip as when he is a newcomer, but any imprudence should always be avoided. More than one minister has been careless and imprudent, and has had cause to regret it.

Personal familiarity with women must be utterly taboo. "A minister, especially a young one, who puts his hands, however innocent-mindedly, on the person of womankind, particularly young girls, is in the mildest language I can command an unmitigated fool," wrote Dr. Barstow.

Visiting the sick

Visitation of the sick is universally conceded to be a prime pastoral duty and one which yields a rich harvest to the pastor conscientiously engaging in it. Nowhere does the minister find himself more welcome or his coming more eagerly awaited than in the sickroom. "The sick are always in," Dr. Clausen put it; and after a time they begin to wonder why their pastor does not hurry around to see them.

As sick people are not, in the nature of the case, normal, so the pastor's visit to them cannot be exactly on a par with that made to a well person. As a general rule the pastor visiting the sick should not give the impression that the situation is a very unheard-of thing, nor "make a fuss" over the patient. Of course the facts should not be blinked. "Here is my friend or my church member, Mrs. Blank, and she is sick in bed, and I have come to see her"—that is a straight-out fact which the minister wants Mrs. Blank to know he knows. But to give Mrs. Blank the impression that a terrible and unusual experience is happening to her is not good. In such situations the attitude of the M.D. can be taken as a model by the D.D. In that splendid address to young physicians, "*Æquinimitas*," by the scholarly Dr. William Osler of Baltimore, the great surgeon put in a plea for "imperturbability" on the part of the physician or surgeon.

Imperturbability means coolness and presence of mind under all circumstances, calmness amid storm, clearness of judgment in moments of grave peril, immobility, impassiveness, or, to use an old and expressive word, *phlegm*. . . . The physician who has the misfortune to be without it, who betrays indecision and worry, and who shows that he is flustered and flurried in ordinary emergencies, loses rapidly the confidence of his patients.

If this is a good rule for *doctores medicae* it applies equally well to *doctores theologiae*. A good doctor brings calmness and a sense of security by his very presence and so should the representative of the Great Physician.

Do not stay long with the sick. James Elmer Russell gave sound injunctions along this line: "One should be as deliberate in entering a sickroom as if he were going to stay all day, but after a few minutes, and certainly before the patient is wearied, and the very sick weary quickly, he should go." [5]

[5] "The Minister and the Sick Room," *Church Management*, May, 1926.

In the helpful little book *The Pastor's Pocket Manual for Hospital and Sickroom,* by Edmond Holt Babbitt, there is a list of "ten harmful things" which the minister should guard against when visiting the sick:

Never ask a patient what his sickness is.

Never sit or lean on the patient's bed. Avoid jarring the bed.

Do not set the patient against the physician or hospital. If there is inefficiency or injustice, go to the proper authorities.

Do not make hospital calls when you have a head cold.

Give no information about the diagnosis even if you know it. It is not your business to tell the patient how sick he is or is not. Information about him will be given the patient by his physician.

Carrying information about patients from room to room belittles your profession.

Avoid carrying worries, problems, friction, tension, crises into the sickroom.

Never enter a patient's room when the door is closed without permission from the nurse on duty. A pastoral call may be needed, or it may be an impossibility. Some patients prefer to have their doors closed all the time.

Never argue with a patient. The purpose of an argument is to win over one's opponent; not to give light. If you disagree, then just disagree, and let it go at that.

Do not ask a new mother if she got what she wanted. It is important that she want what she got.[6]

It is to be remembered when visiting the sick that the patient is the center of the stage. One is often tempted to talk to others who may be present, as this is easier to do; but the sick, like the aged, are hungry for personal attention and should be made to feel that they are more important than anyone else in the room.

[6] Used by permission of Abingdon-Cokesbury Press.

Centering the conversation on the sick will itself demand a short rather than a long visit.

There is an art in leaving properly, and "retreating in good order," to use a military term. This holds in the sickroom as well as other places. Some pastors never master this art, and either break away with a "thank-heaven-that's-over" air, or they sit and sit and mention the fact that they are sorry, but it really is time to go, and sit some more, and finally drag themselves out as though apologizing for casting such a gloom over the room as to leave it. If it is time to go, say so and go.

In regard to prayer in the sickroom, the particular situation in each instance will be the guide. This is the rule which a large number of present-day ministers say they follow. However, a considerable percentage state that they always have prayer with the sick, following in this regard the wise advice of W. Mackintosh Mackay, in his book *The Disease and Remedy of Sin:*

There is a temptation to-day to pretermit bedside intercessions. The minister is afraid lest prayer will terrify the sick man or destroy the natural flow of human intercourse. "Will not a cheerful conversation on secular matters be more helpful than a solemn prayer?" Sometimes, doubtless, it will, and a wise tactfulness must always be used in such cases. But, as a rule, the spiritual practitioner, when he enters a house, should remember that he is not there to perform the *part of an ordinary visitor, but comes to bring spiritual healing.*

It is best for the minister, instead of asking permission to pray, to suggest directly, "Let us have a word of prayer," or "I always like to have prayer with my people (or my friends)," and then proceed to pray. Patients who desire prayer will not always ask for it but will be disappointed if prayer is not made. Certain types of men are afraid that it will show lack of courage if they ask for prayer when they are sick, but they will be secretly pleased if their pastor or ministerial friend authoritatively takes over and asks the blessing of God upon them.

All sickroom prayers should be short.

Of course there are prayers and prayers. Some prayers for the sick were better unsaid—that is, before the sick themselves. For example, one good minister visited an old friend who was ill and, before leaving, prayed for him. He informed the Lord in lugubrious tones that both of them were men living on "borrowed time," that their short and evil days in this vale of tears were fast drawing to an end. The result was much depression for the sick man and much wrath on the part of relatives who had spent weeks of steady cheerful effort to persuade the invalid that he would soon be well. If a postscript were added to this story, it would be to the effect that the relatives in question saw to it that the dear ministerial brother never again got a chance to pray with his old friend. A Christian prayer ought to reflect faith and hope or there is something wrong with the pray-er.

There are certain *times for visiting the sick* which are more appropriate than others. For example, the evening before an operation always finds a man in rather a solemn mood, especially if left in a hospital room by himself. The catharsis through which the physicians put him in order to get him ready for the knife is sometimes carried over into his mental state, and quite often he searches his own mind and considers his own life. He is not afraid exactly—the normal man we speak of—but he is glad to see company or take refuge in a strength not his own. His pastor then, if he has kept up with the state of things, has a very fine opportunity for a helpful visit.

Prayer on such occasions is sometimes more of a problem than in the ordinary sickroom. There must be nothing said or done to induce any additional fear of the ordeal to come. Such would defeat the very purpose of the whole visit, and be no help to the operation itself. Cheerfulness and confidence and hope—let these be reflected in words and bearing and in prayer also, if prayer seems appropriate.

Other good times to visit the sick are when they are about to be taken to the hospital or when they are leaving home in search of health. At other times regular visiting is in order—that is, calls when one is sure the sick will be at leisure to receive. Convalescence is a splendid time, as company is then much appreciated and time hangs heavily.

When a minister first visits a *hospital,* if he is not beforehand acquainted with the authorities there, he should always take occasion to make himself known. This is especially true if one expects to pay constant visits within the walls of that particular institution. The physician in charge, his assistant, the head nurse, the interns, all should be known if constant visiting there is to be a practice. The rules of a hospital should be scrupulously regarded. Usually the minister is permitted some latitude as to hours of visiting, but he should let this permission come from the proper authorities and not take it for granted.

It is important to report to the nurse in charge of the ward at every visit. Although the office may permit one to enter and has given out the information that the man sought for is in Ward E, third corridor on the second floor, it is courteous to report to the nurse in charge of Ward E before entering. She may be dressing a patient in the ward, or for other reasons may not wish a visitor. At any rate she is in charge and her authority should be respected. Most people forget this courtesy and the nurse is correspondingly flattered by the minister's particular knowledge of hospital amenities. She is apt to tell the convalescent patient after his pastor leaves that she likes that kind of preacher. "He knows a lot and seems to be such a good minister." So hearts rule heads, in hospitals as well as elsewhere.

In visiting a ward it is well to speak a word to all other patients who observe the visit. This would be impossible, of course, in large wards; but in a small public ward it is not hard to do, and pleases the pastor's patient as well as the others.

In the case of *contagious diseases* health authorities take charge of the matter of quarantine and have no hesitation in barring the pastor as well as anyone else. But there are times when the pastor can go where he pleases, and must sometimes decide as to whether his visit may not jeopardize the health of others.

As for the minister himself, duty is clear. Dr. Gladden quotes the remarks of Jan Jacob van Oosterzee: "When in 1574, the question here put was expressly deliberated at the Synod of Dort, the answer was given 'that they should go, being called, and even uncalled, insomuch as they know that there will be need of them.' "

All ministers agree on this point. Wherever needed one must go, but carrying contagion must be avoided. A minister who visits in a home where a contagious disease is raging and then forthwith goes into another home among children would receive small thanks from the last-mentioned family. The minister's own home also ought to be taken into consideration, for to endanger his own wife or children would be just as bad as to jeopardize others. Fortunately the contagious diseases usually encountered are not dangerous, and the minister feels that he does well in waiting until the whooping cough, scarlet fever, or measles have subsided among the Jones children; then he may visit them and not spread the epidemic all over town. Of course should great or virulent epidemics come, his service must be given freely regardless of minor considerations. As for the dreaded diseases of maturity—such as tuberculosis—he attempts to visit and serve as best he can, taking all possible precautions to avoid contagion.

When a person is known to be *dying* the pastor should be with him all the time possible. The conversation should be such as becomes Christian people when faced with life's ultimate test. Let faith be strengthened, let hope be in the atmosphere and trust in the prayer. It does not always pay to talk of death except *in extremis* or at the insistent will of the dying. Prayer with the dying is a very delicate ordeal and no rules can be made for it, but many ministers feel better satisfied when they have made a commendatory prayer over the departing.

Dr. Gladden, discussing the ethics of informing the dying of their true condition when they are ignorant of it, took the position that although it is a "hard question" the responsibility of the pastor may equal that of the doctor. It is difficult enough, whoever does it, and neither pastor nor physician is eager for the privilege. Dr. Russell held that the doctor and not the minister should be the one to reveal the situation to the dying.

Next to the sick the *aged* have a special hold on the pastor. We need do no more than mention this fact, but let it be emphasized here that *attention* is what old people want. They wish to be noticed; they wish to be made to feel that they still are part of the world. Some pastors remember their aged members with cards or with occasional remembrances as well as short calls, and such pastors reap a hundredfold. It is not impossible that when our Lord shall call to mind the sick who were visited, the naked who were clothed, the hungry who were fed, he may also add: "I was aged, and ye noticed me; old and infirm, and ye paid attention unto me." Old people, too, are among "the least of these."

Comforting the bereaved

When death comes to a member or a close relative of a member, good pastors go at once to the home affected. It may be that the minister has been at that home but a few minutes before, but let him now return. Death serves as the "you will report at once" order that was so familiar in army days. Of course quite often a minister finds that the person most affected or the one whom he calls to see does not care to receive him or anyone else, but good pastors make their presence known at the door and offer to do anything to help.

Some suggest that the matter of the funeral be tactfully taken up as soon as possible so that the pastor may plan accordingly. It would seem better, however, to let the whole matter of the funeral be managed through the undertaker or relatives. The pastor has no absolute knowledge, or at least may not always presume, that he will be called upon to officiate, though, of course, many times this will be so evident that he can take it for granted. But in general it is better for this to be worked out in private by the family, and the undertaker may then inform the pastor of its wishes. The ministry is called upon to play many parts, it may be admitted, but let us leave to the undertaker his own special work. A funeral is a cataclysmic event in any home, and although it may be arranged at an inconvenient hour the pastor had best leave all other duties and give his unstinted service to those who need it most.

After the funeral the comfort of the pastor's presence is even more necessary than before. While the funeral itself is pending, an excitement, artificial but nevertheless sustaining, prevails in the bereaved home. But when all is over the silence of an aching void begins to bear upon human hearts. It is then that the minister of Jesus Christ can be a true son of consolation. Let him go back as soon as possible—the next day, many ministers advise. The sorrowing wife or father or sister will wish to talk of their great trouble. Let them talk. Most ministers would agree that anything like hysteria should be checked, but wisdom now consists in letting the heart have its say. The minister's sympathetic attitude means more than words can tell. His visits may be repeated at longer and longer intervals, until Time, the great healer, does his work.

Visiting jails or prisons

In the city prisons or large penal institutions an official chaplain is usually in charge of the work among the prisoners. If for any reason another minister should visit any of the inmates, the chaplain as well as the other authorities should be consulted first. The previous suggestions on getting in touch with authorities at the hospital will hold good also when preparing to visit the jail. Prison rules and regulations are more strict than those of the hospital and will be better enforced. The minister should know and observe these regulations.

The minister visiting the prison has the traditional reputation as friend and counselor of the prisoner. In the army the chaplain was for years the legal council for the accused and acted as defense attorney at all courts-martial. This sometimes led, and may today lead in civil life, to the minister becoming such a partisan of the accused that he is viewed with suspicion by the authorities. He is sometimes charged with a degree of sympathy which discredits justice. In most instances this is not true, but the prison visitor should be on guard against the accusation. Men in prison, especially those convicted, stand in the eyes of the people as guilty of crime, and crime is sin. The minister's attitude here must show no compromise, though it must always manifest kindness and the desire to help.

Persons in prison are often possessed by a strange mental

attitude which causes them to blame everyone but themselves for their plight. The judge was unfair, the witnesses perjured, the prosecutor a fiend—and all society was in conspiracy against them. But spiritual redemption for them waits upon the recognition and confession of their own faults, their own sin. It may take courage on the minister's part, and sometimes will require time and repeated visitation to make such a man realize this, but the truth cannot be blinked. "We suffer justly," said the penitent thief on the cross. So says every criminal, who, after breaking the laws of God and man, receives pardon from God but not from man. Shilly-shallying here by the pastor will do harm. Let the prison visitor remember it.

Many courts allow that *confessions* made to ministers and priests by prisoners are privileged communications. A minister therefore cannot be compelled to testify against his will, when his testimony on such matters would act against the prisoner. Such confessions are, of course, inviolable, as are all confessions and confidential statements made to a pastor by his members, whether in jail or out.[7] Dr. Douglas' advice against informing the minister's own wife regarding pastoral confidences is to be recalled: "As a private individual even you have no right to this information."

May a minister ever take advantage of a confession or a confidential statement for the purpose of helping the man who made it? Or to prevent what to him is a wrong? This depends.

---

[7] "The confidential statements made to a minister by his parishioners are privileged and should never be divulged without the consent of those making them." (*Congregational Code*, II, 4. *Methodist Code* identical. *Presbyterian Code* almost so.)

"I will under no circumstances violate confidences that come to me as a minister." (*Disciples Code*, II.)

"It is unethical to divulge the confidences of parishioners without their consent." (*Unitarian Code*, III, 3.)

Faith must be kept at all cost; and if a minister makes a pledge of silence, for instance, and under that pledge receives the confession or confidence in question, he must keep his word. At the same time, to receive a confession or make a pledge binding one's future course without ascertaining beforehand something of the nature of the matters in question is not wise. Unprecedented situations often arise, but the unanimous voice of Christians today affirms that evil may not be done that good shall come. At any rate, a gentleman's word is his bond—and so is a minister's.

Good priests and good ministers who receive confessions indicating that something further needs to be done if right is to prevail are, however, in position to persuade the confessor himself to make the needed move. In certain instances they may obtain his consent to speak or act for him. This has the double advantage of fulfilling a helpful spiritual service on the part of the minister and of allowing the man himself to work out his own moral release by personal decision and action. Also it is in a man's favor with society if he makes confession or attempts restitution himself without being coerced.

Charity and appeals for aid

To deal properly with the whole matter of public charity from a pastor's standpoint is somewhat difficult. When possible, work of this sort ought to be turned over to a social service committee of the church, unless the community has a well-organized system for carrying on such work. It was this very situation which called the diaconate into being in the early church, as the sixth chapter of Acts tells us. The ordinary minister will do well to take a tip from the apostles and escape the obligation of serving tables. The διακονία τοῦ λογοῦ is his special work. However, there are times when the pastor must act as the almoner of his church. If he endeavors to push this matter off on a lay committee he may find that while many needy persons have no objection to a pastor's ministration along this line, they do shrink from having a committee of the church aware of their poverty and need. This, of course, concerns chiefly the better class of charity cases, who are in need but making a struggle. There is another class whose members do not care who knows their condition, just so they are benefited. The whole matter of charity requires special tact and skill. Where possible the pastor does well to see that this is attended to by others who have a special talent for it. In a few cases he will find that he must attend to it himself. When this happens let him see to it that his right hand (meaning the congregation) does not know what his left hand (meaning himself) doeth.

One of our poorer, ne'er-do-well members is at the door and wants to *borrow* some money from us. What about it? Here again circumstances will govern, but all things being equal, which they are not, this business of lending money to parishioners should never be begun. If a loan is made to one member, there is no good reason why it should not be made to others, and the news that a preacher is able and willing to lend money gets around in a wireless but amazing way. This results in loss *to* the preacher and loss *of* the member. There is no person who so sedulously avoids us as the man who owes us money. There will soon be an empty place in the congregation where the fellow sat who borrowed money from his dear pastor, and an equally empty place in his pastor's pocketbook. Most ministers can frankly and truthfully say, when they are thus approached, that they have no money to lend.

Of course there are cases of need, genuine need. These the minister can usually arrange to meet with money from the poor fund or through a church committee. Most ministers, too, quite often place money, their own money, in the hands of the poor; and this is right, for there are times when by every law of God and man a minister must give. When this is the case let it be a gift in the name of Christ. Let it not be called "a loan" unless this is necessary to secure its acceptance. Let it go as bread upon the waters in the work of God.

Ministers have long been considered easy marks for fakes, frauds, and confidence men. However, their reputation along this line is not as "good" as it once was. Yet occasionally some stranger knocks at the minister's door, and leaves him after a few minutes marveling at the fertility of the human brain. The story most commonly told is of a dying relative in a distant place and how the necessary fare to see the loved one is lacking (or partly lacking), followed by a request for a "loan" of the amount needed. Most ministers can supply other versions of this story, and some of the variations are compositions worthy of the great masters. A good way to test such a person is to ask about a minister in the town he claims as home, and if the stranger says he knows him (the Presbyterian preacher or the Baptist, or whatever denomination he may be) to tell him that you will wire or phone and if the local minister indorses him it will be all right. Ministers hear some queer objections to giving this information—doesn't want his town to know his condition; doesn't want to trouble the preacher. Needless to say a genuine fake at this point is glad to *nolle pros* the matter and move on.

Of course not all supplicants are frauds. Food to a hungry tramp, a coin to a beggar—charity is part of the minister's task. "Be not forgetful to entertain strangers," says the writing: "for thereby some have entertained angels unawares." But it is to be very much wished that one might know the genuine trademark of the angels when he sees it and not have to threaten to telephone or telegraph to get a visé on the celestial credentials.[8]

Occasionally agents come with sure-fire propositions for the good of the Aid Society, or for money for the new building fund. In cases of this kind canny ministers are glad to let the Aid Society have them with all their literature and all their works. Ministers have enough to do without engaging in such petty and unprofitable schemes.

It is true, however, that from time to time some exceptional program is offered to a church—a well-known choir on visitation, or a lecturer of note—and there are communities where such would prove welcome. Our ministerial authorities recognize this fact; and while some feel that such programs "rarely prove genuinely helpful," as a New Jersey minister put it, yet they do agree that when one appears to be of high value, some organization of the church may be allowed and depended on to sponsor the occasion.

[8] "A minister should be very careful to protect his brother ministers from imposition by unworthy applicants for aid, and should refer such cases to established charitable agencies rather than to send them to other Churches." (*Presbyterian Code*, III, 5.)

CHAPTER VI

Ministerial Churchmanship

A minister's ethical obligations toward his church can be separated into two main divisions: those relating to his denomination or church general; those relating to his own pulpit and parish, or church local.

Denominational relationships

The minister represents his own denomination or church in the minds of the people. Of late years there has been quite a discussion regarding this representative character of the ministry. Men who find themselves out of sympathy with certain of the doctrines or methods of the denomination whose name they bear have rebelled against the idea that their own ministry should be circumscribed or directed by regulations laid down by others, even by the mind of their own church representatives. Much is heard of "freedom in the pulpit" and of "Christian liberty."

This entire situation can best be judged when one understands the exact status of the relation which every minister holds to his denomination. The following statement should assist in clarifying this matter and will be agreed to by most ministers.

Every minister has entered into some kind of covenant with the church or fellowship which commissioned him. With some this was by vows of ordination in which the minister obligated himself to follow a certain course of conduct, and perhaps assented to a definite creed. With the less centralized denominations the questions asked and the agreement made are not always so definite, but in nearly all Protestant denominations some sort of test or promise is exacted of every man who offers himself as a candidate for that particular ministry. This test or requirement is of course always known beforehand to the candidate, who nevertheless offers himself, and answers the questions to the satisfaction of the denomination or takes the required vows. When this is done the denomination, through its committee, congregation, presbytery, bishop, or council, licenses, ordains, or approves the man and sends him forth as one well fit to preach the doctrine and carry on the work belonging to its particular mission. The church thenceforth relies on the minister's promises, answers or vows. Most denominations never again formally question their ministers. For the duration of a minister's life his church relies upon the obligation once taken or vows once made. This is a truth that is not apparent at a casual glance, but is of supreme importance in viewing this problem. Every minister has promised or sworn himself to a certain course of conduct or discipline through which he became the representative of his own denomination. He was not coerced; he need not have done this; but of his own accord he offered himself, was taken at his word and promise, had a certain stamp of approval put upon him, and was admitted to that particular ministry. Forever after that he is declared unto the world to be a duly accredited minister according to the doctrine, discipline, and polity of his church.

The church after this has the right to expect of him either that he will keep his vows and execute his promises, or that he will terminate the covenant or representative arrangement if he cannot or will not keep it. All churches make provision for such termination of the ministerial status. Either church or minister has a right to end the mutual agreement. The church has the inalienable right which is enjoyed by every sovereign corporate body from the Congress of the United States to the small-town debating society—namely, to act as judge of the qualifications of its own members. The minister, on his side, has the right to withdraw from any organization whose methods or beliefs he cannot indorse. This right to sever relationship, which must be allowed to both church and minister, is not unfair to either, but a safeguard to both. To hold otherwise would be to insist that a great body of believers support and keep as their representative one who is not *in esse* their representative, or to take the equally intolerant attitude that a minister should continue to preach assent to doctrines to which his heart cannot subscribe. There is no more reason for asking a church to place in its pulpits a man whose teaching and beliefs are not in accord with its own than for asking Great Britain to let a Member of Congress from Missouri sit in Parliament. On the other hand there is no more reason for a denomination to expect a minister to serve in its pulpits against his own convictions of right than there is for Congress to pass a law establishing a State religion and compelling all men to subscribe thereto. The way out is clear. Let an irksome partnership be dissolved. The church can then get for herself men who will agree to her beliefs or meet her tests; the minister may get for himself a pulpit with some other fellowship to whose doctrines or lack of doctrines he may agree, or failing that, may gather about him those with similar beliefs and worship with them where he pleases. Henry Wilder Foote has a fine chapter on the liberty of the pulpit in *The Minister and His Parish*, and comes to the conclusion that the minister's liberty is bound by the law of that church to which he belongs. This, the vast number of ministerial authorities agree, is sound and sensible.

The question of *heterodoxy* is at times a troublesome one. A minister may be in agreement with his own church on most or all essentials, but may have his private opinion regarding certain minor points—of doctrine, for instance. It is sometimes said that every man is a heretic at some one point. It is true that all have personal theories or vagaries of thought or fancy; and doubtless there are minor points of belief in which every minister differs from the thought of his own church, perhaps from that of the long line of Christian thinking. Should a man therefore withdraw from his church or insist that such matters deserve the attention of all? Experienced ministers do not believe so. Minor opinions, even doubts of an inconsequential nature, are no part of a minister's message, nor do they injure his work. The rule, "Preach your *dos* and not your *doubts*," is sound. Most ministers, therefore, leave unsolved or perplexing problems out of their public messages, and fail to enlarge upon any difference of interpretation or doctrine which they hold against the thought of their own fellowship. There is no more reason for a minister to withdraw from his denomination because he cannot agree with it upon some minor question of polity or doctrine than there is for a wife to seek a divorce because she does not like the kind of necktie which her husband insists on wearing.

Certainly too much discussion of minor points will not be expedient before the congregation. It is very unwise, not to say wrong, to plant in the minds of the people vague questions and a train of speculations concerning problems over which the best minds of the ages have been exercised. The cardinal doctrines of righteousness and truth are being violated daily, and there is need to preach *them.* Leave speculation alone, say the wisest of the ministers, and preach from the vast reservoir of truth which is filled to overflowing. "But avoid foolish questions, and genealogies, and contentions, and strivings about the law; for they are unprofitable and vain."

But what is to most ministers a minor matter, unprofitable and vain, may become to one man or set of men a question of the highest importance. Such men may believe that to keep silent is to do wrong. If the church will not see this matter in the light in which he views it, such a man may feel impelled to *withdraw* from its fellowship. This has happened numberless times, and there is no discredit to either church or minister when a spirit of fairness and toleration has been mutually manifested. The man is the judge. If he does decide to withdraw of his own accord, he should give formal notice and in an orderly way turn over to the proper authorities all papers, records, and property which he has held by virtue of the connection which he now terminates.

Criticism and disparaging remarks about one's own denomination are sometimes heard from the pulpit. Often this is done in the spirit of the family circle whose members feel that they have the right to criticize each other since they love each other. However, it is not wise nor will it always be understood when a member of either a family or a church publicly criticizes his own. To say the least, it is in bad taste.[1]

Legitimate and constructive criticism is, of course, looked for by every large organization, and these, including churches, usually have constitutional ways for registering the opinion of their own membership and for making any changes that may be deemed wise. Most ministers are profoundly interested in the general relationships of their own denomination and are keen critics of its courses of action. However, most of them consider

---

[1] "The minister should never speak disparagingly of his Church or his profession." (*Unitarian Code*, I, 6.)

it better to effect reforms or obtain changes in policy or creed through constitutional methods. They do not usually go to such lengths as to damage the church by public criticism or threatened withdrawal. Many of the ecclesiastical-statesman type ignore such methods, nor do they issue many controversial statements to the general press. They wait until the time of the council, or convention, or assembly, and then before their peers in conference assembled make the fight for what they hold to be right. Criticism of the general polity of the church when it comes from local pulpits seldom does any good and is embarrassing to visitors.

Disagreement within the denomination may bring up the possibility of *schism*. The question will be asked: What is to be done when no redress for wrong may be obtained through denominational channels? Is one then justified in using extraconstitutional means to bring about what he believes to be right? Shall one, to use a military simile, neglect the "regular military channels" through which protests, and requests, are expected to pass from the lowest officer to the highest (provided no one stops them *en route*) and appeal directly to the powers that be, irrespective of constitutional methods or anything else?

This is the crucial question regarding all rebellion, all revolution. In a measure each case is to be judged upon its own merits and, historically and politically at least, by its results. Martin Luther and George Washington, to name two notable examples, achieved what history declares to have been right by using extraconstitutional means. In the case of the ordinary minister and the laws of his church most ministers are inclined to take the view that the dissenting person will as a rule better achieve his results by working through regular channels than by disregarding them. The man who decides to gain his end regardless of constitution or previous customs, although he may be right under other standards, must be prepared to be treated as a rebel by the organization. It may be observed also that schismatic types as a rule seldom get very far. If they have truth with them, that will eventually prevail; but if they have but a modicum of truth, they will prevail only in a moderate way. Neither churches nor political parties last long when founded upon one issue, and the graveyard of dead churches and political parties will show it. One idea may create a schism, but will not produce an enduring church. In the last analysis, as Carlyle says, every idea must stand in its own strength and get for itself what life it may.

As a rule individuals get further by standing with their organization. Men are intuitively doubtful about the fellow who bolts. There is a certain type in every organization which will rule or ruin, and will not be bound by majority decision. Christian liberty should not be curtailed nor that of conscience, and the man who decides to revolt may do so if he chooses; but let him make up his mind that he is entirely willing to wear the stigma of a rebel before he begins.

Candidature and overture

The whole matter of candidature and overture is of vast interest to ministers in all denominations except those whose men are appointed rather than called to their respective pulpits. Washington Gladden, in his book *The Christian Pastor and the Working Church*, laid down some rules for candidature which present-day ministers agree are still valid. These may be discussed in a twofold way: the seeking of a pastorate by a minister, and the efforts to obtain a minister by a "vacant" church.

It is agreed by all that a *vacant church* has the right to make overtures to whomsoever it pleases, whether the minister in question be attached or unattached, "as no church possesses exclusive right to any minister." It may be imagined, however, that complications and ill feeling may arise when one church is found endeavoring to take away the beloved minister of another congregation. A great deal depends on how the subject is broached, and what sort of spirit is maintained. Present-day ministers agree that one should be passive in regard to such overtures, until of course it becomes his duty to make a decision. Certainly the pastor who obviously has his ear to the ground to catch attractive calls from other places, or who takes pleasure in flaunting before his congregation flattering offers from other churches, will create the impression that he is on the auction block for the highest bidder.

When overtures come to a minister from a church whose pastor has not yet resigned, the universal instruction of the ministry is to let such calls alone. This is absolute.[2] Absolute also is the feeling of the majority of ministers that something more than "private advices" will be required before a man is justified in assuming that a certain pulpit will be vacated. In fact many ministers doubt that even a public announcement regarding a pulpit vacancy gives a man enough on which to proceed—he should be fairly apprised of the situation by interested parties among the church's members before he should formally consent to have his name considered. But others feel that this is quibbling, and that where there is an actual opening any minister may be allowed the right to see that his name is properly put before the seeking congregation.

Ministerial authorities also approve the old rule that "no church should enter into negotiations with a second candidate

---

[2] "It is unethical for a minister to make overtures to or consider overtures from a church whose pastor has not yet resigned." (*Congregational Code*, III, 3. *Presbyterian Code* almost identical.)

"He should discourage all overtures from a church whose minister has not yet resigned." (*Unitarian Code*, IV, 3.)

while it has one before it whose case is not yet determined; and no minister should permit himself to be considered as a candidate by a church until he is positively assured that that church is negotiating with no candidate with respect to whom it has not reached a decision." A minister, of course, may not have the power to forestall overtures from other churches, but the last part of the above quotation he may heed. Ministers shrink from being drawn into a contest with each other for a vacant place, and preserve self-respect better by refusing to strive with one another for an open pulpit.[3] A minister, like a maiden, should insist on being told that he is the one and only person who is in the mind of the wooer—in this case, the congregation.

When the pastor has not resigned and the pulpit is not vacant, no minister worthy of the name will listen to an overture nor make one. The codes we quote enjoin that, but there is another and greater code whose whole temper and spirit forbid a man of God to force out or connive at the deposition of a brother minister. Let no one be deceived. The excuse may be given to oneself, "I can do well that work of God which I see the present incumbent doing so poorly." That may be true but we must allow God to oversee his own work. Certainly no one can possibly bring about good by doing ill.

Where a *minister* decides to seek a church that is vacant it is agreed that he is at liberty to advance his candidacy by any aboveboard and dignified means. The majority of ministerial authorities consulted about this assert that it is better for the candidate not to apply in person, but to get some other party or friends to introduce his name and emphasize his qualifications. There are others who take what they consider a more realistic

[3] "I will refuse to enter into unfair competition with other ministers in order to secure a pulpit or place of honor." (*Disciples Code*, II.)

view, holding that aggressive methods may bring results in a more direct way.

The personality of the man is the decisive factor here, and neither commendatory letters nor hearsay praise will ever equal a ten-minute view of the man in question in the pulpit. On the other hand, what may be all right ethically may be a mistake tactically; and, as wise ministers sometimes say, it is better for the church to seek the man than for the man to seek the church. Ministers, therefore, as a rule deprecate the idea of preaching trial sermons. They urge, and with truth, that a congregation seeking a new pastor should send a committee to hear him while he is at home in his own church rather than invite him to come to theirs. From both the minister's standpoint and that of the seeking church this is the best procedure. The minister, is presumably at home in a well-established pulpit and is not conscious of being tested by alien standards; the visiting group from the seeking congregation has the advantage of judging the preacher by what may be taken as a fair sample of his regular preaching. If nothing comes of it, there is no embarrassment on the part of committee or minister.

There are, however, many instances where this method of appraising a prospective pastor may not be possible. In such cases trial sermons may be not only advisable but necessary. Modern ministers are realistic enough to agree to this, though one writes that there must be no "contest," and another reminds us that trial sermons are a "trial to everybody." The man himself is the chief sufferer, for he wishes to do his best and make sure of success with the people; and yet to give them his best sermon may let the people in for a long term of misgiving afterward if they accept him as pastor, for they will have been shown, not a sample of his preaching, but the cream of it.

In this connection the advice of an old Methodist preacher

who had served many appointments in his time is worth remembering. He said:

When you go to a new place, never preach the best sermon you have the first time you are there. If you do, the people's expectations will be raised so high that you may never be able to satisfy them again. Don't preach your worst sermon either. Just give them a middling good stiff sermon and you have got room after that to go in either direction.

There should be no flaw in the spirit or letter of the title which gives a man a new pulpit and parish. The question is sometimes raised as to whether a man should accept a call when he learns that it is by no means unanimous. About one fourth of the ministers giving their opinion on this subject stated offhand that they would refuse any call unless it were unanimous. However, the majority agree that the whole thing may depend on how large the opposing minority is and what the objections may be. If the objections are such that the minister is sure that he can overcome them, given time and opportunity, well and good. One authority says that it will depend on whether the opposing minority is "reasonable or obstinate." A hostile minority of any kind is a factor to be seriously considered.

When an actual contract is to be signed between pastor and church there usually is no difficulty, once the terms have been understood and agreed upon in advance. It is unthinkable for either minister or church to break the letter or the spirit of such an agreement.

Resignation from one pulpit in order to take up work in another ought to be done in such a way as to safeguard the interests of the work one leaves. Church contracts, where there are such, usually specify that a number of months' notice shall be given by either party desiring to terminate the relationship. At any rate a minister who decides to resign is in duty bound to do so in a formal manner, and should arrange with the proper persons in regard to turning over property, records, and administrative functions.[4]

Mutual rights

In the relationship that exists between a pastor and his own particular parish, pastor and congregation should clearly understand their mutual rights under both church and civil law. Church laws differ in different places, and legal relationships and rights also vary under different charters. Often it takes a factional fight to bring out the exact legal status of mutual rights. Sometimes minister or church has to appeal to Caesar and the *ipse dixit* of a civil judge in a court of chancery finally outlines the rights and obligations of both parties. On such occasions the matter may be settled according to the law, but not according to the prophets—hostility is everlastingly perpetuated. So ministerial prerogatives and oversight, trustees' control and property rights, membership rights, and the like, ought to be understood very thoroughly by all parties concerned.[5]

He would be a foolish minister of course who constantly reminded his people that legally he has this particular right or that special privilege, just as any people would take the heart out of their minister by making him feel that they are suspicious of

---

[4] "The minister's relation to his parish is a sacred contract, which should not be terminated by him, or broken by his resignation, without at least three months' notice, except by special agreement." (*Unitarian Code*, III, 1.)

"It is unethical for the minister to break his contract, made with the Church." (*Congregational Code*, II, 1.)

[5] "The minister is the recognized leader of the parish, but he should not assume authority in church affairs which is not expressly granted to him by the terms of his contract, or the usage of his office, or the vote of his church." (*Unitarian Code*, II, 2.)

his control and must therefore hedge him in with legal restrictions. Nevertheless the minister will do well to know the law of his church regarding his office, the law of the state in which he lives concerning his ministerial rights, and the legal points involved in his own special contract with the local church—if there is a contract.

The *pulpit* is conceded by all as rightfully belonging to the minister. The proclamation of gospel truth is his special mission, and it is also tacitly understood that he must be allowed to have control of all formal worship in the church. Certain churches qualify the pastor's control of the pulpit by stipulated restrictions, but the consensus of opinion holds that the minister should have entire control of it.[6]

To invite into one's pulpit a minister or public speaker who is known to be unacceptable to a great portion of the congregation is of doubtful propriety. Of the ministers queried on this matter, fully half affirmed that it should never be done; the others felt that circumstances might sometimes make it permissible. When the pulpit is opened to one who represents a cause to which many persons in the church do not subscribe—certain types of political speakers, for instance, or those who are pressing for some social action which will not be supported by all—the matter can become acute. The minister should remember that while the pulpit is his responsibility and he must never fear having the truth proclaimed from it, the people, too, have a very real equity in the church and after all are the ones expected to listen. In general little good and often much harm is done by such procedure.

[6] "The minister rightfully controls his own pulpit, but he should not invite persons into it who are not generally acceptable to the parish, and he should be ready to accede to all reasonable requests by responsible church officials for its use" (*Unitarian Code*, II, 3.)

Policies against the temper of the local church should be carefully considered before the minister introduces them. He may be morally right and personally strong enough to force them into effect, but the support of his people is one of his greatest assets. Forfeit that, and the loss is irreparable.

We have already discussed the matter of *the minister's time* from a professional standpoint, but this should be remembered in connection with the local church. A minister may very properly resent the implication that money can pay him for his services, but nevertheless there is a sense in which his time and ability do belong to the local church. No one, of course, tells him how to divide his time, but he should not assume that he is entirely independent of the people who "make the pot boil" for him.[7]

Finances

Laymen are more and more assuming the management of church finances. This is well, and the ministry with a universal sigh of relief will be glad to leave money matters entirely to the membership of the church. Some ministers take an extreme position here and even refuse to allow matters affecting the financial status of the church to be brought to their attention. This attitude on the part of a few pastors does not gain general sup-

[7] "As a minister controls his own time, he should make it a point of honor to give full service to his parish." (*Congregational Code*, I, 1. *Presbyterian Code* identical.)

"When a Methodist minister becomes a member of conference he promises to employ all of his time in the work of God. We again call attention to the fact that he is thus honor bound to give full service to his parish." (*Methodist Code.*)

"He should be conscientious in giving full time and strength to the work of his church, engaging in avocations and other occupations in such a way and to such a degree as not to infringe unduly upon that work unless some definite arrangement for part-time service is made with his church." (*Unitarian Code*, I, 2.)

port. The majority of ministers feel that the laymen of the church ought to be encouraged and helped by their pastor as they carry on their voluntary and sometimes arduous work. Certainly the minister as titular leader of the church ought at least to be sufficiently interested in the struggle his men are making to sit with them as counselor and to keep himself well informed regarding the financial affairs of his parish. However, it is not felt that the minister should actually raise church money himself, except as the public leader in some forward-looking congregational enterprise upon which all are agreed. On the other hand there are ministers who frankly say that they are compelled to lead their people in the matter of raising the regular budget of the church and that they have no hesitation in so doing. The tactful man will know how to help without hindering, be present without dominating, the financial committee of the church.

When *church money* is handled by the minister or when he is made special treasurer of any fund he must be most accurate. Carelessness here is beyond forgiveness. More than once those who have been entrusted with funds for philanthropic or religious causes have had charges leveled against them for improper accounting, and there have been court trials and convictions in certain instances. One noted case of this sort had to do with the treasurer of a reform organization whose plight was brought about, his friends firmly believed, because of poorly kept records rather than criminal intent. Whatever may have been the merits of that case, it is a fact that those who handle money—all philanthropic organizations, committees for relief, etc.—should keep their books so that they may be ready for examination at a moment's notice. Let the minister watch this point carefully, for some have lost pulpits by giving adversaries an opportunity to attack them through their own carelessness.

Church property

The minister should always remember that church property *is* the property of the church. He may very properly consider the parsonage, or manse, or rectory, or pastorium, or whatever his house may be called, as his own property so long as he has charge of that parish. This should be known and appreciated by others, as trouble has sometimes been made by officious church property committees. Nevertheless the most deeply rooted pastor, geographically speaking, will do well to remember that the title to his house is held by others and that he is but a sojourner, as all his predecessors were. This will check him in the matter of taking any unusual steps with regard to church property until the responsible officials have been consulted. The same principle holds also with regard to renting church or even parsonage property for the purpose of gaining additional revenue. The minister who is wise will wish to know how his people feel about such a step before it is taken. The pastor may be well within his rights in renting rooms in the parsonage, but he will save himself some trouble by finding out beforehand how the people view this matter. Church people are perfectly willing to see their pastor made the beneficiary of parsonage property himself, but some have an illogical but strong aversion toward seeing "outsiders" benefit by it. This is a situation that no logic will reach, and the wise minister will take people as they are and not as they ought to be.

Church records

"The records of the Church must be kept with care," affirmed Dr. Gladden. All such records belong to the church.

Protestant ministers, especially of the less centralized denominations, are woefully lacking in this. The Roman Catholic Church can teach some good lessons in preserving records of baptisms and marriages. These sometimes become extremely valuable to the persons involved, and yet few local churches make anything like farsighted preparation for keeping them. The minister must lead in this. He should locate and preserve past records, add his own to these, and keep them for the future in an accurate and systematic way. All records and papers should be turned over to the succeeding minister with careful explanations regarding their nature.

Personal records ought to be kept by each minister and, of course, are private property. Some good system for keeping them ought to be followed. Personal records have the advantage of acting as a check on official records. The sermons a man preaches, when, and where; the marriages he has performed with names, dates, and witnesses; the baptisms (if his church practices infant baptism)—these may be of importance to him and sometimes to others after years have passed.

Publicity

The modern minister is expected to know something of publicity methods and to use them for the benefit of his church. It is the era of the press agent, and church publicity is but a phase of the great science of advertising which America has so well learned. Church bulletins, illuminated signs, floodlighted churches, advertising stunts of all sorts are used by many ministers. Church people take pride in frequent mention of their church in the press, and like to see the name of their minister looming large in the church news section. This is permissible if there is actual news value in such items. Newspapers are glad to get church material when it is really news; and the minister should understand what the local paper may consider of value to its readers and should know how "news style" copy is prepared. It should be remembered also that the Monday morning paper is proverbially more news hungry than that of any other day of the week, inasmuch as Sunday does not provide the general copy that the secular processes of other days provide. Papers will therefore quite often publish with eagerness extracts of sermons, or special events which have taken place in the churches the day before. A copy of the minister's sermon given the paper in advance will often bear fruit in the pages of Monday's paper and may reach even more people than those who heard these paragraphs delivered.

William H. Leach, the editor of *Church Management*, outlined several *rules for publicity* which should guide in advertising one's church.[8] These will be recognized as universally valid:

1. Publicity must be *truthful*. There can be no misleading statements, no exaggeration. As Dr. Leach says:

It [the church] has no right to advertise a great sermon and then have the preacher enter the pulpit to utter platitudes which are already thread worn. It has no moral right to advertise a great musical service and offer a half-baked program which would be barred from any musical test.

It might be added here that even though a church may be able to deceive the people and the press on one or two occasions, this cannot be done often. Truth, like honesty, is the best policy.

2. The advertising must be *subordinate* to the thing advertised. In other words it must be the servant of the church and not the master. This principle will prevent an excessive expendi-

---

[8] *Church Management*, May, 1927.

ture for publicity and keep all things in proportion. When publicity comes to be the chief thing about a church, when in the popular mind the name of that church is but a synonym for freak advertising stunts, or a menagerie, or a fashion show, or a vaudeville, then the church has gone in for a publicity which makes it less than a church. To quote Dr. Leach again:

Laymen have a right to protest when some minister carried away with the glare of notoriety turns the house of God into a public market place. If he must use the tactics of the soap box orator, let him take his soap box into the market place, but when the bell calls folks to the worship of the eternal he should enter into the courts of holiness with prayer and seriousness.

3. The minister cannot afford any publicity *reflecting upon his sincerity* or his character, nor any which makes him appear "as a religious mountebank or freak." Someone has said that the worst comment on the American pulpit is the list of sermon topics which the usual Saturday afternoon paper carries, which pander to the morbid and the sensational. Advertising is lawful if lawfully used, but Truth has a strange way of manifesting itself. The church that is fulfilling its mission soon becomes known for what it is. Lawful publicity is good and no one pleads for the shrinking-violet church, but there is something about the blatant modern way of "telling the world" that is against the drift of the Master's teaching. He had no condemnation for publicans and sinners equal to that which he poured out upon those who sounded a trumpet before them when they gave alms, and who made long prayers in public that they might be seen of men. There may be some warrant for telling the city about the church, but the minister who studies how he may constantly tell the city about himself, his sermon, his

methods, his vacation, his opinions—that man does not fall far short of the ancient ecclesiastics who loved the chief seats in the synagogues, and disfigured their faces that they might appear unto men to fast. Publicity is a splendid thing in its place, and the modern minister should know something about it, but there is something else about which he should know more. Dr. Paul Elmer More of Princeton once lectured to a small group on Greco-Christian philosophy. "The thing the church has lost to-day," said Dr. More, "and the thing it used to have, is this" —and he went to the blackboard and wrote on it:

ταπεινοφροσύνη

which in plain English means Christian humility or, as Archbishop Trench put it, "thinking little of one's self, because this is in a sense the right estimate for any human being no matter how great."

CHAPTER VII

Conducting Public Worship

It is as the conductor of public worship that the minister takes the special place that is his. This is true whether he stands forth to preach or to pray, to announce a hymn or to welcome a new member. What a unique place he now occupies! He stands before his fellow mortals as the representative of the deathless, immortal God; he directs and guides these fellow mortals to worship rightly and worthily praise this God. He furthermore sets the example by his own public action and bearing in rightly representing and worthily speaking for him whom he serves.

The atmosphere of public worship should be carefully guarded by the minister. Charles Jefferson said in *The Building of the Church:*

Blessed is the preacher who converts his church into a temple, and who, with or without pictured windows and without or with the help of ritual and rich architecture, creates by the conduct of the service an atmosphere in which souls instinctively look Godward. ... Atmosphere is everything.

This is true. The atmosphere, the overtone of the congregation gathered to worship God, is different from that found in any other place in the world. Children of the church, strangers, even scoffers, sense that atmosphere instantly. Certain ecclesiastical organizations have carefully studied this matter and make everything possible combine to induce a feeling of reverence and unique position—the windows, statuary, clouds of smoke from swinging censer appealing even to the lowly sense of smell—and whatever heads may say, hearts feel that there is something that transcends the ordinary in the house of God. Hymns, prayers, sermon, even announcements, all should harmonize with and add to this sense of the Presence.

The minister who does not feel this most keenly has had a faint call to what others know for a most sacred office. The man who acts as free and unrestrained in conducting public worship as if he were at a golf match at the country club has not come close to the Almighty. Wretched are the people whose worship is ordered for them by such a man. Like priest, like people. If the minister in the midst of a gathering of worshipers does not feel the presence of the Most High in a unique way, how may the people feel it?

The minister in his pulpit or before his people in the church should be so aware of the sacred and peculiar place that he occupies that the people too will become aware of it and of their own place. The Urim and Thummim of the Lord should shine on the spiritual breastplate of his modern ministers; and when the people feel it, as though some new Sinai be smoking, they will be prepared for thunderings and lightnings and the voice of God. Let the minister before his people constantly remember these things and break not the spirit of worship which belongs to God.

Conduct in the pulpit

Nowhere more than in the pulpit should the minister show forth his best qualities as a gentleman. Not only is he in an atmosphere of worship, but he is also a gentleman in company; and what a gentleman may not say or do in the drawing room must certainly not be done in the house of God.

It is impossible to list all errors in pulpit decorum but present-day ministers feel that the following are especially reprehensible:

Talking needlessly and laughing with a brother minister in the pulpit.

Gazing vacantly about instead of being occupied gravely and intently with the duty of the hour.

Smoothing the hair, arranging the tie, or in any way putting the finishing touch upon one's personal toilet before the congregation.

Touching the face without the use of a handkerchief; blowing one's nose loudly or conspicuously.

Lounging in the chair or pulpit seat; crossing the legs "like a big four," as one man expressed it.

Failing to set an example to the people by absolute reverence in attitude and bearing when someone else is leading the prayer.

Moving needlessly about; showing anxiety over trivial details; "weaving" or rocking up and down on one's toes; putting hands in pockets; dangling a watch chain or engaging in unusual mannerisms; showing a spirit of levity, absent-mindedness, slouchiness, or rudeness in any one of the innumerable ways in which these may be expressed.

There is a correct way to sit when in the pulpit—when in any public company, for that matter. The posture should be erect but not stiff, with feet well under and in toward the chair, each resting evenly on the floor with the heel of one foot even with the instep of the other, and arms close in with hands on the arms of the chair in a natural position. Such a posture gives an impression of respectful and competent alertness.

When a *visiting minister* or speaker is to take part in a regular service, it is customary for the minister in charge to introduce him to the audience. A simple yet gracious introduction is in much better taste than an effusive one. It is well to be explicit as to the initials and title of the visitor and to pronounce his name correctly. If there is a noteworthy fact about him which may recommend him to the audience, this may be stated in brief words. Anything, however, savoring of eulogy or extravagant commendation is always best avoided in introductions, in church and out. Let the speaker stand on his own merits and bring his own message.

When a speaker concludes an address or sermon it is always in good taste for the presiding minister to assume charge again quietly and give the order for the next part of the program. Comment by the presiding minister is risky and difficult. He cannot hope to speak at the point where the other man concluded, and he may mar the spirit under which the audience has been left if he attempts to comment on the message. He may show by his bearing better than his words his own feeling, and by quietly giving out the number of the concluding hymn, for instance, may add to and not break the spirit of the message. If the message has been a good one, the people know it and need not be told; and if it was poor they know that too, and the man who attempts to make them believe otherwise has a task on his hands. It is better, therefore, to refrain from comment after a speech or sermon—though this rule like any other may be broken when occasion demands.

Preparation

The minister feels it a professional duty as well as an ethical and religious one to be prepared beforehand for the conduct of every service. Circumstances, of course, occasionally force the minister into situations where he is able to make no preparation worthy of the name, but the service is always the poorer when this happens. The ministers of all denominations condemn a brother minister who comes unprepared when he takes his place as the leader of public worship.

This matter of preparation is commonly taken to refer to preparation for preaching, but all churches, even the strictly nonliturgical, are coming to place more and more emphasis on the various parts of the service other than the preaching. No longer are we thinking in terms of preaching alone; but, as Dr. Jefferson has it, the whole service from the first note of the voluntary unto the last peal of the organ is worship. So preparation on the minister's part has to do with many things. Does he feel personally prepared? What is his scripture lesson, and will he be able to read it as it should be read? Is he ready to lead the prayers? Fortunately most parts of the church service, like the vital functions of life, become matters of routine—that is to say, habit. Where there is to be no special variation of his regular order of worship the minister is left free to prepare himself for the sermon and other parts that must necessarily be different in each recurrent service, and need not be concerned about the invariable parts of his order of worship which come to be as familiar to him as the fit of his own clothes.

When a special service is to take place, or a special feature to be introduced, all should be carefully arranged beforehand. Suppose another minister is to preach. Details regarding the essential parts of the service should be explained to him in advance. The necessary consultation between ministers should take place before the service and not before the people. Anything that savors of lack of preparation—apparent attempts to select hymns or to settle on a passage of Scripture to be read, etc.—mars the atmosphere of worship.

Preparation for a minister's own part in the worship is not merely a matter of intellectual application or "cramming" on a

sermon outline at the last minute, but rests upon "deeper incon-
sequent deeps." The quiet hour before the service, the prayer
in private, the cultivation of the Presence—these sometimes mean
more than subhead *b* in division III of the sermon. The ancient
church stressed this matter officially, and one of the finest and
best-loved prayers of the Middle Ages, the matchless Collect
for Purity,[1] was given to the priest to say for himself in private

before he went out to the people to celebrate the Sacrament.
Nonliturgical churches, while they have never prescribed any
regimen for private preparation, have always insisted upon the
thing itself—none more so than the fathers of the great evangelical communions.

Many ministers have a *prayer with the members of the choir*
just before a service begins. This has the double advantage of
giving the minister a chance to act as pastor for the members
of the choir, and of impressing upon them the joint responsibility
they share with the minister as leaders in Christian worship.

Order of worship

Liturgical churches have always prescribed a formal *processional* and in this their respective customs and usages are authoritative. Nonliturgical churches also have increasingly
adopted the processional, and here the custom of each individual
church will be determinative. From the minister's point of view
it is desirable to know in advance the exact procedure to be
expected in the church where he is to take part in the worship.

In churches where there is no processional, or where the minister takes his place within the chancel independently of the

[1] Almighty God, unto whom all hearts are open, all desires known, and
from whom no secrets are hid; cleanse the thoughts of our hearts by the
inspiration of thy Holy Spirit, that we may perfectly love thee, and worthily
magnify thy Holy Name; through Christ our Lord.

choir's entrance, good usage prescribes that he keep himself somewhat secluded from the people until the time for the service. There is nothing binding about this and, in small churches and wayside chapels where there is no private room for the minister, it is not out of place for him to wait quietly with the people before "church begins." However, where there is a study or office in the church, usually the minister finds it more convenient to remain there where he may meditate or have a private prayer before he goes to lead the service.

In those churches which do not conform to an ordered processional, the actual entrance of the minister should be dignified but not ostentatious. Henry Ward Beecher said that he abhorred "the formal, stately and solemn entrance of the man whose whole appearance seems to call upon all to see how holy he is." There should be the quiet, natural assurance of one who knows that he is going into the pulpit to lead the people Godward.

Punctuality is a desideratum in beginning a service. Let the minister appear before his people on the stroke of the hour, or a moment or two beforehand—perhaps during the organ prelude, if there is one. In modern churches the pastor's study quite often opens on the pulpit. When there is a visiting minister or ministers the pastor acts as usher for them, leading the way until the pulpit platform is reached, when he steps aside after indicating what seats his brethren are to occupy. The central seat, if there is more than one, is generally assigned to the preacher of the hour or to the guest of honor. Sometimes, however, visiting ministers prefer that the local minister keep the central seat—his usual place—as presiding officer.

It has been traditional for ministers of certain evangelical denominations to bow or kneel for a private prayer after they have entered the chancel or pulpit. Present-day ministers are somewhat divided regarding the propriety of this, many feeling that such a prayer smacks of ostentation. However, others take the position that a man's sincerity must be taken for granted unless there is proof to the contrary. A prominent minister observed that one cannot expect the people to be in a worshipful attitude if the minister is not. It is generally agreed that the custom of a man's church in this regard should be followed.

The actual service in many churches begins with a formal *call to worship*, which may be "said or sung" according to the practice of the respective churches. Where the minister gives the call he should remember that the tone of his voice as well as its strength and inflection has a bearing upon the atmosphere that is to prevail. A certain reverent strength in summons or proclamation is needed, but stridency or explosiveness must be avoided. It is "the silver trumpet," not a brass one, which calls "to holy convocations," according to Christopher Wordsworth's great hymn.

It is the custom in many churches for *hymns* to be announced upon a bulletin board or perhaps by means of a printed bulletin; sometimes scripture readings also are thus announced. The service then proceeds without oral announcement. This is an agreeable practice where the people have been accustomed to it and makes for a smoothly running service. It has the disadvantage of suggesting a certain leaderless impersonality in the worship. Announcement of the hymns by the minister gives him an opportunity to "float" the service along, and to comment occasionally upon the words or music of the hymn to be sung. People respond to helpful public leadership.

When the minister is to give out the number of the hymn let him do it authoritatively and in such a way that all may hear. He may very well repeat the number as there are persons in every congregation who having ears hear not, even when they are listening. Hymns "listlessly announced" were deprecated by

John Barbour when lecturing on "Ministers and Music." He insisted that "the pastor is the leader of the praise . . . The people will always take their key and cue from him. If he slight, hurry over or make nothing of the praise services, the majority of the people will treat them the same way."

An experienced leader of public worship will occasionally give out the number of the hymn, then read the first line of it or call its name, then give out the number again. This is often a good plan. As a rule the minister should let the organ and choir take the hymn as it is written and sing it through. However, for the sake of lightening a service, some ministers adopt the plan of calling for the repetition of certain stanzas, or they exhort the people to sing with more spirit, or call attention, as John Wesley urged should be done, to the words which are being sung. People like to sing, and the wise minister when he sees that they are singing lets them sing on. Choirs and church music are traditionally uncertain factors, and when they are working well, let them work.

When the people are singing let the minister also stand and sing. In *The Art of Preaching* Charles R. Brown had this to say to the minister:

Sing yourself! Do it as a means of grace to your own soul! Do it also as a bit of godly example to your people. The lazy, shiftless minister who announces a hymn and then goes back to his chair and sits down while the people stand up and sing it, as if praising God were no affair of his, ought to be cast out of the synagogue. Unless he is a semi-invalid almost too weak to be there at all, he ought to be pitched out of his pulpit forthwith by some athletic deacon ordained of God as the Scripture says, "to purchase to himself a good degree and great boldness in the faith" by thus exercising his authority as an officer of the church militant.

Needless to say, hymns should be *carefully chosen* with a canny understanding as to what the people know, as well as what may be appropriate for the occasion or topic. Sometimes a hymn which is suitable in language and theme may prove difficult in music; and occasionally a hymn chosen because the first line seems to emphasize a certain theme has many other lines which deal decidedly with other matters. The minister should remember this when he looks for "something appropriate" to go with his message. Fortunately for worship, every good hymn has a unity of its own which transcends and sometimes defies hymnal indexing. A familiar hymn, well sung, is appropriate almost anywhere.

In general the first hymn should be one which is well known by all in order to draw the congregation together immediately in a unity of praise and thanksgiving. New hymns are indeed to be taught the people, and each pastor should have a plan for doing so—but not at the beginning of regular worship. A point later in the service may provide an opportunity to learn a less familiar hymn, or one may be carefully chosen to fit in with the sermon or special theme of the day. It is not a good plan to choose too somnolent a hymn or too lulling a tune just before the sermon. If the people are to be put to sleep, don't let the singing do it!

The last or final hymn may aptly sum up or close the service with a note of aspiration, challenge, or conquest; or it may be one of the robust marching songs of the church. A recessional, of course, does something of this in its own way.

Practices differ considerably in the matter of *public prayer*. The liturgical churches provide fixed and majestic forms of prayer to direct both minister and people in divine praise. In the nonliturgical churches, however, and in all congregations where

146

extempore prayer is used, certain general observations upon this important matter may be made:

I. Prayer is addressed *to God*, not the people. If this is understood, it will keep all prayer reverent, humble, and quiet. John A. Broadus, in his book *Preparation and Delivery of Sermons*, said that in public prayer the minister should "earnestly endeavor to *realize what he is doing.*" He is talking to God. We have all heard prayers which stormed the skies, when the voice and tones of the suppliant made the rafters ring. If this is natural to the man, it is his way of talking and must be respected, but most ministers feel that God will not hear us for our loud speaking any more than for our much speaking, nor do we ordinarily think of him as off on a long journey or perchance asleep. We instinctively feel that reverence is shown by quiet. Dr. Broadus illustrated this by quoting a statement made by R. L. Dabney in his *Sacred Rhetoric*:

The *utterance* of prayer "should be softer, more level, . . . less vehement, more subdued. Every tone should breathe tenderness and supplication. . . . It is difficult to say which is most unsuitable to this sacred exercise—a hurried, perfunctory utterance, as of one who reads some tiresome or trivial matter, a violent and declamatory manner, as though one had ventured upon objurgation of his Maker, or a headlong and confused enunciation."

Since prayer is addressed to God, it is incorrect for the one praying to speak *of* God as a third person. This is sometimes done and there are a few ministers who state that they do not consider it wrong; however, the overwhelming number hold that it is. Certainly it seems incongruous both logically and devotionally to refer to God in a prayer to God.

Long English usage has always prescribed formal address and use of the formal pronouns when man purports to talk with his Maker. It is "thou," not "you," which respect seems to demand from those who have been taught to pray either at home or in church. Naïve and uneducated people sometimes adopt the more familiar *you* in addressing the Deity, and they should not be criticized inasmuch as anyone's form of prayer must be respected. But for the ministry as a whole the ancient usage seems far more agreeable in public worship.

Those who use the formal language of English prayer should be careful about their verb endings when the second personal pronoun is being used. It is "thou" who "hast," not who "hath"; who "lovest," not "loveth," etc. Reading the well-furnished liturgies of the past will help a man in this respect as in many other ways.

Since in prayer man addresses God, he should not at the same time attempt to address the audience or put out ideas for purely human consumption. "To pray for another minister present with elaborate compliment, is a sadly frequent, and grossly improper practice," Dr. Broadus affirmed. Anything in prayer that savors of making a speech to the audience, or getting off information for the benefit of the congregation is bad. No true prayer can be filled with didactic affirmations and thou-knowest-this and thou-knowest-that tidbits of human news gathering. Prayer is unto God.

Dean W. L. Sperry holds that the great fault of extemporary prayer is didacticism, or giving information for the benefit of men rather than God. As he put it:

The informational serpent in the grass . . . is forever creeping into extempore prayer. We are all aware of this liability, . . . yet how hard it is to keep clear in pastoral prayer of that mental process by which we give information either to God or to the congregation. Once we start with the preface, "O God, thou knowest . . ." or

"O God, we are gathered here together, and thou seest . . ." the serpent has raised its head in our Eden.[2]

2. The minister prays *for*—that is, in behalf of and in place of—the entire congregation. This should keep him from expressing his own private feelings or emotions too decidedly. Since he is the mouthpiece of all, any tendency toward giving way to personal sentiments or expressing his own opinions should be carefully watched. In this regard thought and study beforehand will help the minister lead the people. Some of the most prominent preachers in the country state that they put almost as much time on studying their formal pastoral prayer for each Sunday as they do on the sermon they are to preach. Presbyterian ministers have traditionally set the rest of the clergy a good example here.

Pulpit prayers can become "grooved" before the pray-er knows it, and many a nonliturgical minister who refuses to be guided by a "book of prayer forms" unconsciously drops into a prayer pattern which is as fixed as anything in the Prayer Book and far inferior in language and thought.

3. Prayers should not be *long*. If anyone wishes to disagree with this statement it may be amended to "prayers should not be *too* long." Asked about the length of their pulpit prayers, present-day ministers show quite a difference of opinion. The average length is between three and five minutes, with some making it "four to six," some "five or seven," one or two suggesting "anywhere up to ten minutes." But the "long pastoral prayer" of earlier days has definitely been much shortened. George Whitefield once rebuked a man who prayed a long prayer by saying: "Sir, you prayed me into a good frame, and then you prayed me out of it."

[2] *Religion In Life*, Summer, 1933.

Prayer is not expected to take the place of the sermon in formal worship. Dr. Nathaniel J. Burton tells of a minister who told the Lord so much in an opening prayer that the speaker of the occasion had no thunder, and not much heart, left. Prayer has a field all its own in both public and private worship. Happy is the man who can commune with God in the presence of his people.

The correct posture in prayer has always been a debatable matter, and the custom of a man's church is to be respected in each instance. Prayer ought, of course, to be audible to all, and, as Dr. Broadus warned, hands are not to be placed before one's face nor should the head be so bent down as to stifle utterance. "We must also avoid contortions of countenance, and tricks of posture and gesture, which there will always be some persons to notice."

With the advent of the pulpit microphone and amplifier systems in churches more point is given to the injunction regarding audibility in prayer. As the microphone is almost always on the pulpit, the minister must stand for his prayer as well as his sermon.

Scripture readings should be selected and studied beforehand. Public reading of the Scriptures is not always easy, and to do it well familiarity with the thought as well as the words is essential. It is, however, a richly rewarding part of the service, and people long to hear the Bible read so that it may speak its own message to them. Good authorities suggest that pronunciation should be carefully studied, and where "indelicate expressions as we see it" occur, these may be omitted, or expressed according to some different version.

Commenting upon the scripture lesson while reading it does not please the majority of ministers polled on this. "Give it to the people unvarnished," they say; "let the Word be its own witness." But quite a number take the other position and say that it is perfectly all right for a minister to comment as he reads if he feels so inclined—that he is "an expounder of the Word of God." All agree that ambiguous or difficult turns of expression may profitably be explained when a word or two will suffice; and many ministers who say that they never comment on the Scripture while reading it advise taking time to "give the setting of the lesson" before they actually begin to read.

As a rule, obscure scripture lessons are to be avoided. All scripture should be read slowly and impressively so that the man on the back seat will be able to understand.

Responsive reading calls for a technique all its own. The minister "sets the pace" and also the tone by reading the first line, couplet, or verse. The leader may err either by going too fast, or by picking up the first word of his sentence before the people have completed the last of theirs. This jumping ahead on the part of the minister communicates a certain jittery feeling to the responsers and makes for uneasiness. A good leader will know how to set a verbal pace that will be strong and sure, yet not too slow, and will thus guide the people to do their part more evenly.

A great many ministers open *the pulpit Bible* reverently when they first come into the pulpit, and close it reverently as the service ends. But there are others who state that they wait until the actual time to read the lesson before they open the Bible, and that they close it when the lesson ends. Others say that they keep the Bible open at all times, that it is never closed; while still others see that the Bible is open as the service begins, and let someone else, presumably the sexton, close it after all worshipers have gone.

Protestant churches find something symbolic in the open Bible. It is the charter and warrant for all that the Church stands for. While a crass bibliolatry is not to be implied, all agree that casual or thoughtless treatment of the Bible, such as slamming it about or banging on it, is forbidden by reverent good taste.

The giving of *announcements* is part of the service in practically all churches today, although a printed bulletin often provides an ideal medium through which this may be done. Announcements in church are not new in the history of public worship, for the Church of England in the first Prayer Book of Edward VI four hundred years ago had a rubric calling for the priest to announce what holy days were to be kept, what marriage banns were to be published, etc. It is not, therefore, to be considered a "break" in ordered worship when the modern minister takes time to announce some special event or to emphasize some particular duty. However, announcements which are trivial and trite will sometimes seem to interrupt the even flow of a service of worship; and where a printed bulletin is provided to take care of such matters it should be depended upon to do so. Otherwise let the minister make all announcements worthy of public notice in a dignified way.

In some churches it is the custom for a lay officer to make the announcements on the principle that temporal affairs and the mechanics of church life are properly under the management of the laity. Announcements if made at all should be made well. When announcements are printed in a bulletin, any public reading of them is a waste of needed time. However, while ministers all agree that this is a good rule, many admit that they break it from time to time when some particular matter needs to be especially emphasized.

Since there is a stated time for announcements, they should be made at that time and not interspersed throughout other parts of the service. It is not wise to emphasize an announcement or repeat one just before the benediction. While the people's heads are bowed in quiet for the final blessing, such an announcement breaks into the peace in which they should be allowed to depart.

Taking an *offering* in church is another custom of great antiquity, and has long been firmly entrenched as part of the service among American Protestant churches. Some churches dislike the public passing of the plate and prefer other means of securing funds. Private subscriptions or even a box for contributions at the door of the church are sometimes substituted, but the time-honored passing of the plate is not likely soon to disappear, and the people as they give their gifts have an opportunity to participate directly in the service.

When a public collection is taken it should be done quietly and efficiently. The laymen of the church usually have this matter in hand, and it seems more in keeping with the spirit of the offering for one of the laymen to supervise it and stand as representative of the church while it is being taken. However, in certain of the liturgical churches the clergyman manages these matters, and the presentation of the alms and offerings is a formal ministerial act. As different churches have different methods and ceremonies connected with the taking and receiving of the offering, no more need be said upon this. It should be remembered, however, that the offering is and should be a true part of the people's worship, and when carried out in that spirit becomes a blessing to the givers.

Some have felt that the minister should put his contribution in the plate like any other person in the congregation. This is rarely done and would be difficult to arrange without causing the minister to appear either awkward or ostentatious.

Every minister should of course give what he can to the church budget and see that his contribution reaches the church treasurer regularly. He should do this out of his own salary and as his personal contribution, not as something previously "allowed" out of a hypothetically larger salary. Ministers have sometimes been criticized for their failure to see that their own personal financial contribution is at least as large as that of any other person of equivalent salary in the congregation.

The sermon

There are many able and comprehensive books upon preaching, and both the preparation and the delivery of sermons have been treated exhaustively by competent authorities. Certain major principles are involved, and the minister would do well to heed a word or two of general caution.

When a man preaches let him be *natural*. This is the injunction of all experienced ministers as they speak to their younger brethren. There must be no imitation of another, no cant, no "holy whine"—let every man be himself. If God has truly called a man, he will have a message to be delivered through his own personality, speaking in his own way.

Cant is the bane of all genuinely religious people. "Good Lord, deliver me from cant" was in one preacher's private litany. This is the way all sincere ministers feel, and it is unnecessary to do more than mention it here. A caution might be put in, however, that since the use or repetition of phrases which are meaningless to an outsider or casual hearer will sometimes lay a minister open to the charge of cant, he had best avoid such phraseology, no matter how well he understands it. This charge disappears when the genuine character of the man or of his message is known, but it always pays to speak in a tongue that the people can understand.

Chief faults in sermon delivery as listed by prominent ministers are: using a "holy tone" or any unnatural voice; "oh-ing" and "ah-ing"; poor enunciation; studied oratory or dramatic

154

effect; yelling and pulpit pounding; inaudibility; following notes or manuscript too closely; singsong delivery; explosiveness; rising on toes; walking about too much; oscillating from one leg to the other; acrobatics; facial contortions, looking at ceiling or floor instead of people; failing to obtain "eye directness" with people; preaching to front half of congregation or to those on one side rather than to all; using hands too much; holding gown with both hands or putting hands in pockets when preaching; preaching not for a verdict but for approval or to get through; prolonging the conclusion.

There are, of course, many other faults which might be listed, and personal mannerisms are almost as numerous as persons. Of mannerisms, however, it may be said that some of these may actually enhance the attractiveness of a popular speaker or beloved pastor, as they seem to belong to the essence of the man; but any mannerism which continues to call attention to itself rather than to the man or the message is bad.

A different sort of technique is called for in preaching *before a microphone*, not only when the minister is "on the air" but when, as is often the case in churches today, there is an amplifier system in the church or even earphones for those hard of hearing. Good broadcasters tell us that the microphone is the "ear" into which all speech is directed just as though the whole audience were only these few inches away. One does not, therefore, pitch his voice to reach the man on the back seat as he must do when preaching without a microphone. Faults to be avoided are moving the head so as to vary the distance between the mouth and the microphone, as even the slightest variation is magnified enormously in the sonic result; and changing the voice abruptly, as in a sudden shout, since this will likewise be magnified far beyond normal.

Someone asked Henry Ward Beecher once what he thought

of *sensational preaching*. He answered that he was against it, if by it was meant a low temporary success by mere trickery; but if it meant "preaching which produced a sensation" he was for it. His meaning is clear—the gospel itself is revolutionary. "These that have turned the world upside down are come hither also." The Thessalonian Jews had it right—the world was, then as always, turned upside down by direct, personal, unequivocal preaching of the Cross. To that extent the minister must be a sensationalist. But the studied effort to supply people and press with sermons and opinions merely to cause comment or gain crowds is not only forsaking the highest ideal; it means trouble for the man himself. A preacher who starts out that way must "go himself one better" each Sunday. There is enough truth in the gospel to provide all the sensation any man may consistently inaugurate and sustain, but claptrap methods and gaudy attempts to "catch the crowd" have but one end—they run out, and their promoter usually is compelled to run out with them.

Personal mention in sermons should be carefully handled. There is an instinctive reverence for the preaching of the Word which the ages have taught people to feel; and it is not always wise to encroach upon that reverence by pulling in little details of local interest or adding personal allusions which are commonplace in the minds of the people. On the other hand sometimes these local references are easily understood and serve to fasten the thought of the sermon in the minds of the hearers. It is a matter upon which every man must judge with an individual evaluation each time. Jesus certainly dealt with everyday life. Personal allusions, however, or those narrating adventures and opinions of the speaker must be watched, lest the appearance of egotism be given. Ministers everywhere agree that personal references are to be used very sparingly if at all. Most ministers of taste ask pardon of the audience when a reference to a personal experience is to be made or when some intimate picture of self or of one's family is to be drawn. Of late years this request for pardon is not heard so frequently, although personal narratives and opinions have by no means decreased. It ought, however, to be done and will serve the double purpose of gaining the good will of the audience and at the same time acting as a check on a minister's too frequent use of such allusions. The calling of personal names, references to persons in the audience by name, etc., is not considered in good taste. In fact, in legislative bodies and all public assemblies of a formal sort, the use of names is avoided. It is "Mr. Chairman," or "the gentleman from Mississippi," or "the chairman of the committee," not "Dr. Jones" or "Senator Smith." The same atmosphere of formality holds in public worship, and the "reading out in meeting" of private names is to be avoided where possible.

The *use of slang* ought also to be watched. Slang, since it is a linguistic outlaw, is all the more powerful, and many a minister sometimes resorts to it to drive his point home in an unforgettable way. Yet its use should be guarded, for if it becomes habitual its power will be weakened, like a whip to a horse, and the antipathy felt toward it by the "purists" in the audience will overbalance its value as an effective instrument.

Scolding people, especially those present for those absent, is in bad taste as well as bad temper. In fact no minister or public speaker should ever show himself piqued at the size of his audience, and as a rule one does better to make no comment at all upon the number present. If the congregation is large one may act as though large congregations are of course expected; if the audience is disappointingly small he flatters those present by giving them his best and acting as though they are equal to a great multitude.

A minister should not *correct disorder* in such a way as to

157

bring about greater disorder. It should, however, be said that a minister will do well to see that his service of worship is treated with respect by all present. If disturbing noises outside the building can be eliminated by a request from the laymen of the church or by other authority, the minister is right in demanding that his people suffer no interruption from that source. Likewise when interruptions or disorder occur in the audience during the service or during his sermon he serves both his people and his message by seeing to it that this does not continue. The best plan is for the minister simply to stop preaching or stop the service until perfect quiet reigns, then go on. A pause of half a minute is usually sufficient. No comment need be made; just wait for quiet. It will not be long before the persons responsible will take the hint and either sit in quiet or cease to appear in that particular church. Fortunately it appears that disorderly conduct in church—talking, laughing, etc.—has disappeared with the cruder manners of an earlier pioneer day.

Taking a message of another and giving it as one's own is known as *plagiarism*. It is condemned by all ministers and defined differently by all. However, the honest minister will know when he takes what is in reality the work of another. All ministerial codes and ministers everywhere condemn plagiarism, though they recognize that all men are indebted to those who have spoken or written before them, and that often the thoughts and minds of the great leaders of the Christian pulpit must perforce be followed. But indebtedness for general thinking or even for a special approach is one thing, and taking the direct words or the individual sermonic creation of another is something else. No exact rule can be given which will truly and exactly define plagiarism, but when a man feels compelled to take the message or words of another, he should be careful to give due credit, or at any rate to indicate that his thinking has at this point been directly influenced. [3]

Conclusion of the service

A formal *ascription* closes the sermon in certain liturgical churches, and in the nonliturgical there is often an extempore prayer. This should be brief and devotional and, of course, in line with the general theme of the discourse.

It has long been the custom to "let the people go" with a *benediction* that will complete the service and perpetuate as much as possible the atmosphere of worship. Whether this benediction is given from the pulpit or elsewhere, as at the conclusion of the recessional, will depend on the pattern of worship followed by the respective churches.

In many churches there is provided an opportunity for momentary silence or *meditation* after the benediction. During this meditation the people, of course, remain in their places. The organ may play softly a few bars during this meditative period and after that the entire service is over.

Some ministers encourage their people to leave the sanctuary immediately and quietly after the service of worship has been concluded. Others feel that the easy exchanges of greeting among the people and the talk of friend with friend as they prepare to leave are a part of the "communion of the saints" and not to be frowned upon. Christian fellowship is certainly as sacred as any formal part of a Sunday's worship.

It is a widespread custom among churches for the minister to stand at the door of his church and greet the people as they

[3] "It is unethical for the minister to use sermon material prepared by another without acknowledging the source from which it comes." (*Congregational Code*, I, 5. *Presbyterian* and *Methodist Codes* identical.)
"I will not plagiarize." (*Disciples Code*, I.)

leave. A few have felt that greeting the people at the door seems to imply the desire on the minister's part to be complimented on his sermon. However, the vast majority of pastors are thinking far more of their church and their people than of themselves at this time and realize the opportunity they have of doing an amazing amount of pastoral work as their people pass by them. A handshake here, a word of inquiry about an absent loved one, a comment on some matter of personal interest, a welcome to a visitor—all such reap a rich pastoral reward. Some ministers, of course, have more ability at this sort of thing than others but a warmhearted "doorway pastorate" can be made most effective. Naturally if the weather is inclement or cold the pastor will wish to stand where he will not suffer from its effects, but common sense will dictate how one may be shielded by a door or wrapped for the necessary protection.

CHAPTER VIII

Funerals

A minister in charge of a funeral finds himself in one of the most difficult of situations. He represents God, under whose watch-care all events, even death, take place; he represents humanity in its efforts to assuage the bitterness of the hour; and at the same time he represents his own ecclesiastical organization, his own profession, in conducting a public service. The keynote of right conduct in all these various relationships will be found in quietness and a calm, assured attitude in both voice and bearing. Anything that breaks into the calm surety of the atmosphere will be a hindrance to the proper conduct of this service. This is the general guiding principle. Loud or strident tones, harsh singing, or even expressions which break in upon the peace of death should be carefully guarded against.

Church funeral

If the funeral is held in a church, quite often there is a *processional*. The officiating minister usually meets the body at the church door as the pallbearers bring it up the steps. He may have been waiting in the pastor's room until the moment arrives, or he may have remained unobtrusively by the church door while the people gathered. His conduct should be quiet and reverent. There should be no unnecessary talking or movement on the part of anyone.

It is the custom of some ministers to go first to the home of the deceased and accompany the funeral procession to the church. This gives an opportunity for a private prayer with the family before the formalities of the actual funeral begin. But the great majority of ministers reporting on this matter follow the time-honored English usage of "meeting the corpse at the church door and proceeding before it"—that is, into the church.

In the processional itself the minister or ministers precede the body down the aisle while one of them reads such words as his church may provide for the occasion, or as he himself selects. When processional sentences are read, this should be done in a distinct but not overly loud tone. The reading should cease about the time the body is placed before the altar or pulpit or "chancel rail." The minister has, of course, by that time gone on into the pulpit or wherever he is to stand during the service. When several ministers are present they march by two in the procession, and the one who reads the sentences goes in front of all.

Where there is no formal processional—and many churches and ministers do not favor one—the minister either accompanies the family to the church and then makes his way unostentatiously into the pulpit or chancel, or waits at the church and goes into the pulpit slightly before the service is to begin. Then he commences the service with readings or prayers, or perhaps there is music. In some instances the minister walks in the processional but does not read any processional sentences. Certain ministers and denominations look with less favor upon the reading of processional sentences than upon the actual processional itself.

As to *readings and prayers*, the occasion calls, not for trumpet blasts, but for the quiet and soothing pronouncement of the magnificent words which from time immemorial have been the consolation of the bereaved. As different churches have different selections, no more need be said at this point.

Where extempore prayer forms part of the funeral service the minister will wish to be more careful of his words in this than in any other formal prayer. He must not wound the feelings and susceptibilities of the grief-stricken, nor must he do violence to his own conceptions of the providence of God. Usually even the nonliturgical ministers gradually evolve in their recurrent ministration their own "funeral prayer," and this with minor variations they repeat at each funeral. A truly sympathetic pastor will have no trouble in suiting himself to each occasion of this sort. In *The Making of a Minister* Charles R. Brown advised that the funeral prayer should not be too long.

Concerning *singing* at funerals it may be said that such hymns as are used must, of course, be in keeping with the occasion. A few well-trained voices are much better—a quartet, for instance —than a large number of singers. The whole program for a formal funeral should be worked out carefully beforehand, and a number of copies of the program may well be made out and given to those who are to take part. Then when a hymn is to be sung, the minister in charge, with a nod to the choir, may so indicate. Likewise the other ministers who have been asked to take part will the more easily fulfill their duty at the designated time without need of spoken announcement. This makes for a more orderly and reverent service than would harsh announcements.

The practice of preaching a formal *funeral sermon* is now generally discontinued. It came to full strength a generation or two ago in the evangelical churches of the United States, but as it led to numerous abuses and absurdities the traditional "funeral sermon" has now almost disappeared except in certain localities. However, about half the ministers reporting their practice in this regard state that they make "brief remarks," or usually have some sort of short homily or message of comfort as part of their service. Others state flatly that they simply read the funeral service and let the august words of Scripture and of Christian hope be the message.

In the traditional funeral sermon of the past ministers were commonly expected to eulogize the character of the departed, and so ran the risk, as John A. Broadus said, of giving "the lie to all their ordinary preaching." [1] Every minister, of course, wishes to comfort the bereaved and to say what good he can of each person whose life's record he is called upon to close; but honesty and candor must not be forfeited in the process. The impersonal phrases of the burial service are certainly much better than the attempt to steer between the Scylla of family grief and the Charybdis of the majesty of the judgment of God. For watching this dangerous feat of navigation and inwardly commenting on it are always to be found an array of persons who knew the late lamented far better than the officiating minister. Let him therefore either stick to the written form or make remarks of a general nature which stress the timeless verities of the gospel. For it must also be remembered that other funerals are yet to be held, and the minister who goes "all out" for one person's father or husband or son or daughter will have other sons or wives or fathers or mothers facing him with their dead in days to come. If he has been extravagant in his remarks about the excellencies of one of his members, he will be expected to be as generous with others. It is for these reasons that ministers of experience state that they use a printed office and avoid all personal remarks if possible.

[1] *The Preparation and Delivery of Sermons.*

It must be admitted, however, that where a pastor in a few words can tactfully say something which will serve to individualize the particular person whose funeral is being conducted, his brief sentences will be remembered and appreciated by the family and friends more than all the rest of the service. Some ministers make a point of securing from the family a few facts about the life of the deceased—birth, family record, date of death, etc. This was the way Washington Gladden advised doing it, weaving these annals into a brief message of hope and faith.[2] Broadus said that when references are made to a person at a funeral they must be *"scrupulously true,* though not necessarily *all* the truth, for this would often be superfluous and sometimes painful."* He advised that when the departed was a Christian that fact should be stressed.

The funeral rite in church is generally closed by the statement, "The service will be continued at the cemetery," or, in the case of a private interment, a mention of that fact. The ministers then leave the pulpit and precede the coffin up the aisle in a slow procession. The people should quietly stand and wait until the family, following the pallbearers, have left the church. In the meanwhile the ministers have preceded the body to the funeral car, where they stand while the coffin is being put in place. When the doors of the funeral car are closed upon the coffin they may then seek the places provided for them in the funeral procession.

Immemorial custom prescribes a certain order in the position of the clergy, undertaker, pallbearers, funeral car, and family in a funeral procession. The undertaker as the one in charge of such matters indicates to each participant what station he is to assume in the march. Usually the undertaker leads the proces-

[2] *The Christian Pastor and the Working Church.*

sion, as he should, in order to clear the way and indicate the route to be followed. The clergy come next, preceding all but the directing undertaker.

When the funeral party arrives at the cemetery the minister should go at once to the funeral car, where he stands as a sort of guard while the flowers are being taken to the grave and other preparations made. When the procession starts he of course precedes the body to the grave and takes his station while the coffin is "made ready to be lowered."

During an outdoor processional and at the interment itself it is almost instinctive for men to remove their hats and thus honor the dead. This is an understandable custom in pleasant weather, but most people do not feel that the living ought to be jeopardized for the dead. Dr. Gladden agreed here and stated that the men should be admonished to keep their hats on when the weather is cold or inclement. The undertaker usually takes care of this matter, but if he does not the minister may well say to the pallbearers, "Let us keep our hats on, gentlemen," and set the example. Sometimes the hand may be put to the hat brim in a semimilitary way and thus give the desired expression of respect.

The prayers and readings given in the open air may be spoken in a stronger way than within a building, but the tone of quiet firmness should not be dropped.

The *committal*, which is the heart of the final service, was formerly objected to by many as savoring of a priestly commendation. The Presbyterians for a long time would have nothing resembling it; and John Wesley, when he gave a prayer book to American Methodism in 1784, deleted the committal from his office for the burial of the dead. Methodism, however, in the middle of the nineteenth century replaced the committal in the burial service, and many manuals in use among Presbyterian preachers call for this ceremony if desired. Dr. Gladden expressed a well-balanced Protestant view when he said that the English committal service is almost identical with that employed in German Lutheran churches and "is always appropriate." There seems to be no special objection to it today in Protestantism. The wording, even in the Prayer Book, has been so altered that no warrant may be found for the statement that commendation implies any more than does the whole ceremony of Christian burial.

Present-day ministers are almost unanimous, however, in feeling that the committal should be said by the pastor of the deceased if he is present, and the service is usually so arranged. The first part of the outdoor service—known in the English Prayer Book as "anthems at the grave"—may be assigned to an assisting minister, and so may the benediction, but ministers all agree that the committal itself belongs to the pastor.

A slight majority of the ministers approached on this subject indicate that they object to the "ashes to ashes, dust to dust" phrases of the traditional committal. The ground of their objection, as expressed by one man, is that the previous service has been one of hope but now "as clods are thrown upon the coffin the ominous words 'earth to earth' bring our heavenly thoughts down with a shudder and we go away with a heavy sense of having left our loved ones in the cold ground." The spirit of the objection may be understood and every man must do what seems best. Their tougher-minded brethren see nothing to cavil at in this regard, since the traditional committal does not so much emphasize the "dust to dust" expression as it does the majestic expectation of Christian consummation and hope. There are various forms of this committal prayer, and ministers of nonliturgical churches can easily evolve or find for themselves a prayer which seems suitable to them.

Home funeral

The funeral service at the house of the deceased has become of late years much more common than the church funeral. It may be conducted along the same lines as described above, but is somewhat less formal. The same hints, however, as to a program prepared in advance may well be taken. The minister usually finds out ahead whether he is expected to use his own car or whether the undertaker will send for him. In the latter case (and it is the one which entails less trouble) it is best to arrange to get to the home very near the appointed hour. While the undertaker is in actual charge of all arrangements, it is the minister who is popularly thought of as being in control. He should conduct himself accordingly. It does no good to stand about the home for a considerable time before the service begins.

Often when the minister arrives the members of the family ask to see him. In most cases the minister finds that some special request or some final wishes are then made known. Occasionally he is called upon to speak to the sorrowing for the purpose of consolation. Here the quiet assurance of an intimate prayer with the members of the family can often be of inestimable help. Great tact, however, and something like canny wisdom is often called for on the part of the minister. For before the service the people of the house are keyed up for the ordeal; guests are present, and sometimes curious onlookers; and this may force artificiality on the part of the home people. In a few instances there will be relatives whose grief is partially assumed. They feel that everyone expects them to show how much they cared for the loved one by "carrying on"—and carry on they will. Ministers occasionally stumble into a situation of this sort. In such cases it sometimes happens that people who enjoy loosing the emotions really work themselves up into hysterics, or faints; and the minister is called, sometimes repeatedly, to labor with such persons.

If he diagnoses this situation rightly, he can, by prompt and firm—not to say stern—words, call for peace, and get it too. "Among rude, untaught, excitable people," said Dr. Brown, "these expressions of grief may readily carry them over into something hysterical. The minister is there to induce a calmer, saner, more Christian way of facing death." Of course sometimes a genuine and deep grief calls for and extorts expression. It is then that only God can help, and upon him his minister must lean in these moments.

At a funeral home

What has been said regarding the church funeral and the home funeral is applicable to the service conducted in an undertaker's chapel, or "funeral home." Somewhat less formal than a church, somewhat more so than a private residence, these institutions have come to be a feature in modern life. Naturally the undertaker prefers that each funeral he is called upon to manage shall be held in his establishment, as he has arranged and appointed it for that special purpose. The clergy and the churches have been the more ready to acquiesce in the use of funeral homes since the heating of the church building in winter, the summoning of the janitor, arranging for the organist, etc., require administrative time, effort, and expense. And as a private residence is not usually large enough nor suitably appointed for a public ceremony, the funeral home has, understandably enough, come to supplant both church and residence.

There is, of course, no processional in a funeral home, for the body is usually resting in state there. The minister takes his station at the pulpit or lectern and begins with readings and prayers. The service is somewhat more brief than that at a church, though the minister may always profitably remind himself that each funeral is the *only* funeral to the particular people who feel its dread visitation.

There is quite often a brief processional out of the funeral parlor in which the minister leads the way to the funeral car, or he may proceed at once to the funeral car to stand there while the body is placed in it, or in some situations he goes directly to his own car to be ready for the journey to the cemetery.

Special services

When a *fraternal order* is to have a part in a funeral, such part should be clearly understood beforehand by all participants, including the minister. When a family asks a minister to conduct a funeral he may very properly assume that he is in charge of all the ceremonies connected with the event. He will, of course, wish to be as considerate as possible of others who may also have been invited to take part. Misunderstanding and embarrassment may sometimes occur unless there is a complete understanding beforehand regarding the part each is to assume. Common sense, not to say common sympathy, can usually be depended upon to work out such matters. The tactful minister will have no trouble in making the lodge or veteran's organization feel that it has an essential part in the program, and they should in turn respect his pastoral position. As a rule good fraternity men are easy to work with—that is why they are good fraternity men—and there need never be any conflict over management of details.

Ministers are called upon from time to time to participate in formal *military funerals*. These may be extremely elaborate, and those who have served as chaplains in the armed forces can testify what a rigid part protocol plays in such events. In the usual instance—the reburial of an overseas casualty or the death of a local person whose comrades wish to give him a military funeral—all details affecting the part the minister is to play in the service may easily be ascertained beforehand. Where an elaborate state funeral of some high-ranking officer is to be held, the military or naval marshal in charge may be depended upon to give the minister—whether in uniform as a chaplain or out of it as pastor—his direction and cue in each instance. The dramatic salute of the firing squad, if one is present, and the final sounding of taps by the bugler come after the chaplain (or minister) has pronounced the final benediction.

Memorial services are sometimes called **for.** The chief difference between a memorial service and a regular funeral service is that the body of the deceased is never present at a memorial service, and this forces a somewhat different pattern of procedure. None of the mechanics or movement of the usual funeral is in evidence, and those conducting the memorial rites must center their service and remarks definitely upon the person memorialized. Generalities will not do here—the whole occasion is for the purpose of remembering and paying tribute to a certain individual person. Fortunately memorial services are seldom requested and seldom held unless the person in whose memory they are held is worthy of public notice and esteem.

Relations with undertakers

The minister and the undertaker share a joint responsibility in the management of a funeral. Theoretically the clergyman has full charge of the rites and ceremonies in their spiritual significance and import, and as the conductor of an act of public worship he has also a certain additional authority. The undertaker has charge of practical details and the mechanics of all events connected with the entire funeral occasion. Both men are public functionaries and both, of course, must work together. While there have sometimes been complaints by ministers about officious undertakers who overdramatize their professional function at funerals, most ministers see the undertaker as one who is sincerely trying to serve people who are in trouble, and is endeavoring to perform his professional services in a helpful way.

CHAPTER IX

Marriages

Marriage is a rite which from time immemorial has been esteemed a religious one. In ancient times the priest or minister was the sole judge as to who might be married, for there was no state license as at present. The priest or clergyman proclaimed "the banns" in public for a specified period, so that if there was any objection on the part of anyone, it might be stated and evaluated beforehand. If no objection was brought, and if the proposed marriage was in accord with the laws of his church, the priest or minister would then marry the couple. In all cases the priest was the judge as to the right of matrimony.

Now, however, the state has come in, and the minister is no longer under the necessity of acting as a court to ascertain and proclaim the right of marriage between persons. The state's license clears the minister of civil obligations, but he is not clear of his own spiritual responsibility in this matter. The large denominations have made regulations governing the conduct of their ministers, but it may be said that the only situation in which the matter becomes acute today is in the remarriage of certain classes of divorced persons.

Divorced persons and remarriage

A large section of the Protestant ministry has always held that the "innocent party" to a divorce granted on the grounds of adultery might very properly be married a second time to another. Ecclesiastical regulations of certain Protestant denominations have so allowed, though there have always been those who maintain that while divorce is permissible, and even necessary in some instances, remarriage is not. "A divorce *a mensa et thoro* [from bed and board] gives all needed relief," Bishop Charles Fiske once said in defending this latter view. But of late years there has been a definite liberalizing of remarriage-after-divorce regulations on the part of certain large Protestant denominations. The opinion is gaining ground among ministers that a marriage may be broken by other sins than adultery.

Dr. Newman Smyth in his *Christian Ethics* held that there were sins which were "the moral equivalent" of adultery in disrupting marriage—habitual drunkenness, for instance, which "may utterly destroy the spiritual unity of a home and threaten even the physical security of one of the persons bound by the vows of marriage." The Methodist Church allows her ministers to remarry the innocent party to a divorce whose "true cause . . . was adultery or other vicious conditions which through mental or physical cruelty or physical peril invalidated the marriage vow." Supporting this general attitude, though not these special regulations, are ministers of many faiths who have increasingly come to feel that the right of remarriage on the part of any divorced person is something that may not be dealt with by a general regulation, but by careful and considerate attention to each individual case. But no matter how they differ as to the rules followed, ministers everywhere feel a sense of solemn concern toward the whole problem of divorce and remarriage.

When a minister is asked to remarry a divorced person three possible procedures are open to him:

1. The minister can refuse to remarry any divorced person *whatever be the circumstances*. This is the rule followed by a

comparatively small number of ministers. It does not commend itself to the vast majority.

2. The minister can *follow scrupulously the special ecclesiastical law* of his church touching this whole matter. About one third of the ministers reporting their practice toward remarriage after divorce state that this is their procedure. Where church law is specific and directly applicable, ministers who owe it allegiance should be guided by it. The law of their church is their warrant, or their excuse, as the case may be.

3. A minister can *examine each case on its own merits* and, in the light of the best knowledge he can get, decide whether it is right or wrong for him to remarry the divorced person. This is apparently the practice of the great majority of Protestant ministers and of two thirds of the ministerial authorities relied upon by this book. Many of these, of course, belong to denominations which do not provide exact regulations in this matter. Perhaps they may belong to the less centralized denominations which cannot press upon their ministers any special rule or discipline. Some have the right under their church law to determine whether or not "vicious conditions" have broken the previous marriage of the presumably "innocent" party who now seeks remarriage. Naturally any minister who undertakes to pass upon the ins and outs of a divorce case has a tremendous responsibility thrust upon him. He may make a mistake whatever he decides to do.

In this situation the best course is to ascertain all the facts bearing upon the first marriage and the conditions which broke that marriage. Was there a genuine first marriage? Has there been an annulment or a divorce? How long has the divorce been granted? What do the legal papers say regarding the cause of the divorce and the time when remarriage may be allowed? Above all what do the people involved say? for a private personal interview which deals with actual facts and which makes clear the intent of each person involved—rather than legal processes or public hearsay—will give the minister his best guidance. Then if he decides he may not conscientiously remarry the involved person, he should say so, courteously and gently, but frankly and definitely. If on the other hand he decides to go ahead, let him do so, not grudgingly nor half doubtfully—the time for doubt is over—but as graciously and helpfully as he would for any other marriage. His faith in the couple and expressed belief in their future may go far toward launching them into a well-founded new life.

Protestant ministers are not always aware of the ecclesiastical distinction between *annulment* and divorce. An annulment is a legal or ecclesiastical pronouncement stating that no valid marriage has ever taken place between two persons and that the supposed marriage between them is null and void. The ancient church worked out a whole series of regulations bearing upon this matter and outlined the impediments which nullify a marriage. Blood relationship between the contracting parties within "forbidden degrees" of consanguinity; failure to consummate a marriage physically; insanity, if it be proved to exist before marriage, as this keeps the afflicted party from entering into a valid marriage contract (but if insanity occurs after marriage neither annulment nor divorce is allowed as this comes under the "for better, for worse" vow); the existence of a previous unbroken marriage—these are among the causes for which the state and the ancient churches allow annulment. The Roman Catholic Church, so strict on divorce, allows remarriage after annulment but remains the judge as to the validity of the annulment. As state law and ancient canon law differ in some respects regarding annulment, the Protestant minister, who may not feel himself bound by either, will wish to review all facts in every case. Nevertheless, if he determines that the state has acted rightly in granting an annulment, he may remarry the party concerned. Sometimes he may find that a person has been given a divorce rather than an annulment, as the former was simpler to obtain; and divorces have frequently been obtained by collusion between the parties when real causes have been concealed beneath pretended ones. The minister must in all cases get the actual facts, and act in accordance with them.

Elopements

Runaway couples sometimes come to the minister to be married. When the parties are entirely unknown, the minister should be quite careful before he consents to give his services. A candid conference between himself and the parties, sometimes between himself and the intended bride alone, will often make the situation clear. Many sagacious ministers state that they refuse to perform runaway marriages under any circumstances, though others feel that if the parties are properly qualified as to age and intelligence, and seem to know their own mind, they may well be married.

Elopements today, however, are decreasing as the various states of the Union have become stricter in regard to the issuance of marriage licenses. Many require a certain time to elapse before a license can be used. Also there are, in some instances, regulations as to health and blood tests which must be fulfilled before a marriage license is granted. These moves have served to discourage the flight of thoughtless and unprepared couples to the nearest Gretna Green. Ministers should remember, however, that occasionally there are couples who want to "slip away and be married quietly" for perfectly proper reasons—often financial.

Ethical responsibility

The state will not and cannot force a minister to marry a couple against his will. Its license is an authorization, not a mandate. When a minister marries a couple, therefore, he may not escape responsibility for his act by saying that if he does not, another minister will. This is simply to recall the Master's "it must needs be that offences come" and to forget the latter half of that pronouncement.

No minister worthy of the name should ever give the impression that his marriage service is simply a formula for a fee. "Marrying parsons" have brought discredit upon the whole Christian community and upon marriage itself in some localities. Those ministers who take part in freak marriages or perform the wedding ceremony in some spectacular place or manner are guilty of degrading an awe-ful and a sacramental act.[1]

Preparing for a marriage

The minister will do well to remember that he is regarded as master of ceremonies at every wedding. Until he has pronounced the final blessing all must wait upon him. This is cited not to present the minister as one who is in a class with the bride, or even the groom, in public regard, but to make clear his responsibility until he finishes his part. "Marriage consultants"—a highly specialized profession found occasionally in large cities—family advisers, etc., may play a helpful part in the mechanics of a wedding, but the clergyman is in control of the actual service

---

[1] "The minister should be careful not to bring reproach on his calling by joining in marriage improper persons." (*Congregational Code*, I, 7. *Methodist Code* almost identical.)

"I will not be a party to funeral or marriage rackets." (*Disciples Code*, IV.)

"The minister is not under obligations to marry every couple that comes to him to be married. The power of refusal, however, should be exercised with great discretion." (*Unitarian Code*, V, 1.)

itself. He should never let the occasion "get away from him." The time is traditionally one of gaiety, especially in a home wedding; but anything like lightness or levity on the part of the minister, especially before the service, will detract much from his office. A gracious dignity is the key to his whole demeanor.

The minister is expected to be an authority on everything connected with a wedding and is often referred to for advice upon minor points having to do with the occasion. Thus he may find it advisable to obtain an authoritative book dealing with the proper procedure at a formal wedding.

The bride-to-be customarily fixes the time and hour for the wedding, and the pastor of the bride is usually asked to officiate. This, however, is not a fixed rule, as it may be that either bride or groom has a close relative who is a clergyman, or one who is so closely tied to one of the families that he, rather than the immediate pastor, will be selected for the occasion. In such circumstances the wise pastor will of course understand. It is courteous in such situations for the parties to invite the pastor to have a part in the service.

The groom is expected to call upon the minister a short time before the wedding day and formally request his services. If the bride has already learned from the minister that he will be available for the wedding, the groom really has no more to do than complete the arrangements.

The groom is supposed to provide a conveyance for the clergyman when he must go some distance to the church or home, but since today most ministers own their own cars the offer of the groom is frequently refused with thanks. When there are two or more ministers taking part in the service, one old-fashioned rule of etiquette held that the conveyance should call first for the lower-ranking clergyman, then for the higher. No attention would be paid to such today.

Where the wedding is to be held in a church and is to be somewhat formal, there is usually a *rehearsal*. The minister as well as the organist and sexton is expected to be present for this, though it is not always possible for extremely busy pastors to be with the wedding party at the rehearsal. In such cases the pastor should delegate an assistant or other helper to represent him and to indicate just what the minister's part is to be in the service. It is highly advisable, however, that the pastor attend the rehearsal if at all possible, as he will not only get to know the entire group in a much more intimate way by so doing, but will be able to induce a sense of security and ease by the assured way in which he directs the arrangements. The bride-to-be traditionally does not take part in the rehearsal, some other person acting for her. She is, however, in position to criticize and make suggestions regarding the arrangements, and her mentor or consultant likewise may have advice to give.

Where the minister is looked to, as frequently he is, for the proper direction of the entire rehearsal, he should at once assume charge. He may well begin by having the party posed *en tableau* before him, just as they will be when he is to begin the ceremony; then, having got their respective positions in mind, the parties may go to the back of the church, the minister to his station by a side door, and the marches can commence and be repeated until all is satisfactory.

A church wedding

The church has been for ages the place where matrimony is solemnized. In England, we are told, marriages rarely take place elsewhere. In our country the home wedding is quite frequent, but most formal weddings are solemnized within a church. The church of the bride is the proper place for her wedding, even though she expects to leave it afterward for that of her husband.

Where the church is small, as in a village or rural neighborhood, or where the minister has no assistant, he may find it necessary to give orders to the sexton regarding opening and preparing the church for the wedding occasion. This should, of course, be done in plenty of time and the sexton instructed to be on hand at least an hour or two in advance to take care of necessary arrangements. The ushers for a formal wedding should be on hand forty-five minutes or at least a half hour beforehand, though their instructions come from the bride and groom.

An examination of the marriage license by the minister ought always to precede final preparation, if for no other reason than to see that the form is properly made out. Where the parties are well known to the minister he need not be as careful in this matter as he must be when he faces perfect strangers, but carefulness always pays.

It will be supposed that the ushers have managed their duties well, and that the wedding party has arrived at the anteroom of the church, where the bridesmaids are throwing off wraps and putting the finishing touches upon their costumes and that of the bride. In the meanwhile the minister with the groom and best man is in the vestry room or pastor's study awaiting the opening chord of the organ. If there is no pastor's study or private room, the pastor and groom may stand by a side door or remain in concealment until the minute arrives for them to take their respective places.

At the proper moment the sexton throws wide the doors for the wedding party, or the signal agreed upon is given, and the wedding march peals forth. The minister walks slowly to take his place within the chancel facing the audience. Most ministers take their station before any of the bridal party have reached the chancel. A few ministers, however, state that they take their place just after the ushers have reached the chancel. The minister makes no attempt to keep step with the music as the ushers and bridesmaids do. He is followed at a short interval by the groom and best man, who stand at his left, half turned, watching for the entrance of the bride. It should be emphasized that the whole group forms on the minister—that is, with respect to his station—and his position is thus a guide to that of the others. When the bride arrives on the arm of her father, the groom usually takes a step or so to meet her; she releases her father's arm and puts her hand in that of the groom, and both take their places before the minister. He in turn advances a step toward them, "book in hand." The bride's father then steps back and stands behind and to the left of the bride; the bridesmaids and groomsmen "close in" slightly; and the ceremony begins.

Ministers usually have their own manuals, rituals, or prayer books directing them in the proper conduct of the marriage rite; and even ministers of those denominations which do not prescribe any fixed office gradually evolve for themselves a regular form which they use at each recurrent service. The usual ceremony, however, is that based upon the Office for the Solemnization of Matrimony as ordered by the Prayer Book of the Church of England. The Protestant Episcopal Church in America has retained this office with some changes in the interest of brevity and delicacy of expression, neither of which was very pronounced in the Old Prayer Book. The same office slightly abridged was transmitted to the Methodist Episcopal Church in America by John Wesley in his famous "Sunday Service," or Methodist liturgy of 1784. Through the Church of Scotland this Anglican office also reached various Reformed churches, such as the Presbyterian Church, U. S. A. This ancient office thus became the rite for a large group of American church people, and has been the base of nearly all revised or individually evolved services. Lloyd C. Douglas once commended this ancient rite as the only one. "You will find," he said, "that all these home-brewed rituals lack a great deal of the dignity, power, and charm of the service to which I have referred." Hence in order to outline the marriage service in the following pages we may trace the successive steps of this ancient and august ceremony.

From time immemorial the position of the man and woman when they are standing before the minister has been the same, "the man on the right of the woman and the woman on the left of the man." This means that the woman is upon the right of the minister and the man to his left as he faces the couple.

The *address* with which this office opens is a general one and should be spoken to the entire assemblage in a sure yet gracious way. It is usually considered best for the minister to hold his ritual, manual, or prayer book in his hand and make occasional reference to it. He should be most familiar with the service and able if need be to repeat it from memory, but the book itself seems to give something of official dignity and sanction to his act. Dean Charles R. Brown expressed himself strongly against this in *The Making of a Minister*, advising that the marriage ceremony be learned by heart: "The impressiveness of a marriage ceremony is greatly increased where the minister does not have to be looking back and forth from John and Mary to the pages of the book or glancing occasionally from the book into the faces of the bride and groom." But the majority of ministers today—about 75 per cent of those describing their custom in this regard—do not agree, and state that they always "hold the book."

There is a *challenge* at the close of the address in the ancient office, one that demands that if there be any who can "show just cause why they may not lawfully be joined together, let him now speak." Since this is a sweeping challenge, it should be addressed in a general way to the audience.

A *challenge to the parties* next follows. As this is to the couple only, the voice and look of the officiating minister are directed to them in a more intimate and personal way as he inquires if they "know any impediment" why they "may not be lawfully joined together."

In recent years the challenge to the audience and the challenge to the parties have both been omitted by some from the marriage office, on the principle that the couple would not be standing there if they had not already satisfied both the civil authorities and their own consciences that there was nothing to prevent their marriage. But those who defend the ancient use here say that a marriage is all the more valid if it can be certified afterward that neither the world (represented by the audience) nor the parties, solemnly and publicly questioned, knew any objection regarding it.

Since no reply in either case is anticipated, the minister at once goes into the *espousals*. This is the familiar, "Wilt thou have this woman to thy wedded wife . . . ?" The given names are used—"John, wilt thou have this woman . . . ?" "Mary, wilt thou have this man . . . ?"

Anciently the espousal or espousals preceded the marriage, sometimes by years. They corresponded in medieval times to what we now should term "engagements." The espousal is the mutual promise and expression of willingness on the part of each person to take the other, and "keep only unto him" so long as both shall live.

Next in the ancient office comes the ceremony known as "giving away the bride," or in more formal language, the *"giving into marriage of the woman."* The father or nearest male relative usually performs this service, though his participation is chiefly concerned with escorting the bride to the groom. This ceremony is not to be regarded as an outgrowth of the old custom of coemption, or buying of the bride by the groom, though some have contended that this was its origin. But the language of the churchly office makes it plain that the father does not give his daughter to the man but *to be married* to the man. He gives her to the Church, represented by the clergyman, who in turn marries her to the man. The old York Rite from which this ceremony was taken and incorporated into the English office makes this plain: *Deinde sacerdos*, "Who gyves me thys wyfe?" The "wife" was given to the priest, who married her to the man.

In keeping with this idea the father, when the minister asks, "Who giveth this woman to be married to this man?" steps forward and symbolically places the hand of the bride in that of the minister, who at once places it in the hand of the groom. Some rituals today, for example the Methodist, provide an office in which the father responds, "I do," when this question is asked. The Protestant Episcopal use, and that of the Church of England, has never called for an audible response on the part of the kinsman who gives the bride in marriage, the symbolic giving of her hand to the minister and to the groom fulfilling this requisite. Until this part of the service the father has been standing a half step behind and to the side of the bride. Now after putting her hand in that of the minister, the father steps back to take his place with the bride's mother, or kinspeople, in the seat provided.

It is at this point that the true *marriage*, technically speaking, begins. In keeping with this idea the officiating clergyman—that is, the one who is actually to *marry* the couple—now takes the service, if he has not had it from the beginning. Where there is another minister to assist, such an assistant is often given the conduct of the office up to this point—that is, beginning with the marriage address and through the giving into marriage of the woman. The majority of ministers who report their custom in this regard state that they so divide the service. However, quite a few state that they frequently assign the wedding prayer (in the last part of the service) to an assisting minister. Some ministers report that this whole matter of dividing the marriage office is a matter of indifference to them. Thus they say that when more than one minister is to take part in a wedding, let the two divide the service in any way which seems mutually agreeable. But ancient usage, powerful even among the nonliturgical ministers, calls for the actual marriage, that is the plighting of the troth and the pledging with the ring, to be conducted by the clergyman in charge.

Ministers should understand the dramatic movement which underlies the successive steps of the marriage rite. The audience has been called to witness by the address; the parties have been challenged for obstacle; the espousals have been heard; the father has given away the bride—now the actual marriage may begin. In keeping with this idea it has long been the custom of the clergymen of the Church of England and of the Protestant Episcopal Church to turn at this point and, followed by the couple, proceed from the nave of the church up the steps to the altar. There the couple again stand before him and the rest of the rite takes place. Clergymen are divided regarding allowing others than the actual wedding couple to approach the altar, though a slight majority of those reporting their practice state that they do allow the best man and maid of honor to accompany the wedding couple to the altar. The bride must dispose of her bridal bouquet in order to have her left hand free for the ring, and the maid of honor can be of assistance to her at this point; while the best man is traditionally the keeper of the ring for the groom.

Most nonliturgical churches have no facilities for this approach to the altar, as the chancel rail has no gate or opening, nor is there an altar arranged as in the English or Protestant

Episcopal churches. Hence in nonliturgical churches, or those with a center pulpit, the entire ceremony takes place before the chancel rail.

The *betrothal* now takes place and consists in a symbolic taking of hands and the repetition by each party of a betrothal speech: "I John take thee Mary . . ." The printed rubric or general practice of each church governs in this matter, but it is often convenient for the minister himself to join the hands and, if he chooses, to keep his own hand lightly upon the clasped hands of the bridal pair while they are "plighting troth." In outlining the respective speeches of the couple here, as well as in the "ring ceremony," the minister had best proceed by short phrases rather than long ones.

The *wedding*, or "ring ceremony," is a very ancient part of the marriage rite. In medieval times the ring was blessed by the priest after the man had said, "With this ringe I the wed, and this gold and siluer I the geue, and With my body I the Worshipe, and With all my worldly cathel I the endowe," and then put the ring upon the woman's thumb saying, "In the Name of the Father"; and then on the *secundo digito* (second finger) saying, "and of the Son"; and then on the third finger saying, "and of the Holy Ghost," and then upon the fourth finger saying, "Amen." Because of the blessing of the ring as done in medieval times, the Puritans objected bitterly to the ring ceremony and the old Presbyterian Directory appeared without it. So also John Wesley removed the ring ceremony from the marriage rite which he transmitted to America, and not until comparatively recent times did Presbyterians or Methodists in America replace this ceremony in their rituals. The Protestant Episcopal Church, of course, always had it and in 1928 put in an optional prayer for the blessing of the ring. The Methodist Church since 1940 has inserted a little speech to be made by the minister regarding the ring, and an optional prayer blessing, not the ring, but the giving of it. Most nonliturgical ministers today have no scruples against the "ring ceremony" even where their own service books do not include it. It is in reality a beautiful and symbolic act.

Those who follow strictly the intent and direction of the ancient office and its rubric in the "giving and receiving of a ring" arrange it so that the ring itself makes a circle among the parties involved. The ancient rubric outlined these steps: "*The man shall give* [1] *unto the woman a ring. . . . And the minister, taking* [2] *the ring* [from the woman] *shall give* [3] *it to the man to put* [4] *it upon the fourth finger of the woman's left hand. And the man holding it there and taught by the minister shall say . . .*"

The ancient rubric has been modified within recent years, so that there is no mention of the woman's receiving the ring until the man puts it upon her finger. The minister takes the ring from the man directly, blesses it, or affirms regarding it, or perhaps with no words at all gives it to the man to put upon the woman's finger. In this ceremony the minister again "teaches," that is, outlines the words the man must say.

It is interesting to observe that the name "wedding," which properly belongs only to this ceremony, has been generalized to mean in modern parlance the entire marriage rite. As was indicated above, for a long time the Presbyterians and Methodists solemnized many a "marriage" that was not a "wedding." Emily Post misses it when she states that when a couple is married in a parsonage or rectory they may have "a marriage" but never "a wedding." Whenever the groom weds—that is, pledges—the bride with a ring, there is a wedding. A "wed" was a pledge in Old English, and a wedding was of course a pledging.

In case there is a double ring ceremony, the giving of the

ring by the woman follows immediately her wedding by the man. The manner in which the man's ring is given may be exactly duplicated in the giving of the ring by the woman.

The *wedding prayer* follows. Quite often, as has been indicated, when there is more than one minister, this prayer is given to one who is assisting. However, as a rule it is better, once the officiating minister has taken over the service, for him to proceed to the end, as the wedding prayer is very short and the pronouncement that a marriage has taken place and the final blessing really belong to the one who is chiefly responsible for the rite.

After the wedding prayer there is a symbolic joining of hands again for the *pronouncement of marriage*. A great many ministers at this point prefer to clasp together the joined hands of the couple while saying, "Those whom God hath joined together, let no man put asunder," and then proclaim to all the fact of the marriage: "Forasmuch as John and Mary have consented," etc.

The couple usually kneel for a final *blessing* or benediction by the minister, which he may give with uplifted hand.

When they arise, the minister may congratulate the newly married pair if he wishes, provided that he does so in such a gracious way that the solemnity of the service which he has just concluded will not be impaired. Then the organist begins the march, and the party goes out in reverse order from that in which it entered.

Inquiry as to how long a minister should remain "in position" after a formal wedding is over brought a great variety of answers from ministerial authorities. Some few leave at once; a larger number go when the wedding party is well down the aisle; while a still larger number say they wait until the family has begun to withdraw. In all cases the minister goes out unobtrusively and of course never goes down the aisle as a part of the wedding recessional. Sometimes the bride and groom and their wedding party remain in the foyer of the church for a few moments of informal reception as their friends leave. This is a custom that has much to commend it for those who do not find it possible to invite all their friends to a postwedding reception.

Double wedding

A double wedding, sometimes planned when sisters are the brides, is unusually difficult for the minister. There are portions of the service which he may adapt and use for both couples, but portions which most specifically must be individualized—not to speak of four given names to remember, and these four to be properly matched at the crucial moments. Also the rings—certainly two, perhaps four!

Usage calls for the senior sister and her groom to stand to the left of the minister, the junior sister and her groom on his right. He marries the older first.

The address, with a slight adaptation, may be read for both couples—"met to join together this man and this woman [nodding to the left couple] and this man and this woman [nodding to the right] in the holy estate of matrimony." Separate challenges must be given for each couple, and the espousals require a definite question to each of the four persons; likewise there must be a separate giving in marriage for each pair. The betrothals of course are managed separately, and so are the weddings. The wedding prayer, with an adaptation to the two couples, can be read for both, but the pronouncement of marriage must be entirely separate for each couple. The benediction or blessing can be adapted for both. The minister will be glad when it is all over.

Home wedding

A home wedding may be made almost as formal as one in a church if so desired. "Some semblance of a chancel, flowery bower, or canopy is arranged at the end of the room reserved for the ceremony." The minister usually prefers to keep himself somewhat in seclusion until time for the marriage. Generally a room is assigned to him and other gentlemen guests of the groom. He should give himself enough time in advance to examine the license and arrange last-minute details with the parties.

At the appointed moment he takes his station at the designated place. The couple with attendants, etc., come in with a formal march, or in a less formal way if they have so decided. The details of the service as outlined in the church wedding may act as a guide here. Quite often it is arranged to have a reception for the bride and groom immediately after the ceremony; and when this is the case, the minister, after congratulating the couple, yields his place to them. They turn to face the company and receive the congratulations of their friends.

Minor details, such as filling out the marriage license, etc., may be attended to in a careful way after the ceremony. A much less formal atmosphere pervades a wedding reception in the home, and the minister usually feels free to enter into the spirit of the occasion as any gentleman might.

Marriage at the minister's home

Often marriages take place at the minister's home, and in such cases he must not only be the officiating clergyman but also the host. His wife may help him welcome the couple, and also she may act as witness when the law requires a witness.

The minister's duty in dealing with runaway weddings has already been discussed. Let is be supposed, however, that he feels free to marry the couple who are now in his living room. He will have the two stand together, their friends and attendants, if there are any, behind them. The ceremony is conducted while all stand, as there are no facilities for kneeling even if one's particular service calls for the couple to kneel. The blessing may be given with uplifted hand and then the couple allowed to depart after the necessary papers have been filled out.

CHAPTER X

Ministerial Dress

The whole matter of proper dress for the minister may very well be left to the instincts of a gentleman, but when a man belongs to a church or ecclesiastical order which expects him to wear a distinctive garb, he ought to wear it. This is the sum of all that might be written upon this entire subject.

Many ecclesiasticisms have their own regulations or, what are sometimes even more powerful, their own customs prescribing the garb in which their men are to appear. This creates good use for the ministers involved; and it can be said here that no matter how formal the occasion may be, when a minister is dressed in his usual clerical attire he is always considered to be in perfect taste. As is the case with military and naval officers, whose uniform is proper for any appearance they may make, the clergyman's distinctive garb is always correct.

For ministers of the nonliturgical churches, or those who do not wear any special garb, the ordinary three-piece sack suit with the usual accessories for everyday wear provides a costume which is in keeping on all usual occasions. As is true for any gentleman, one's clothes should be inconspicuous; and the minister will not choose any suiting that is striking or unusual. "Parishioners are not eager to have their preacher wear showy apparel," Murray H. Leiffer reports in *The Layman Looks at the Minister.* The same study makes clear, however, that people do not care for somber clothes on their pastor. Dark blues or dark grays are always "safe." Ministers as a rule are not able to have more than one all-around good suit. That one therefore should be of the best, and so chosen that it will be appropriate on any occasion—in the pulpit, at a funeral, a wedding, or wherever the minister must appear in his public capacity. The same rule holds in choosing an overcoat.

Formal ministerial costume

Certain churches have their own regulations and customs which prescribe the wearing of *vestments* for occasions of formal worship and church ceremonies. The use of such vestments is of course authoritative for the ministers of these churches, and no further comment need be made.

The *pulpit gown,* or clerical robe, sometimes referred to as a "pulpit robe" or "Geneva gown," has come to be used for formal pulpit wear almost universally by the ministers of the larger nonliturgical denominations of the North and West, though not so generally by ministers of the South. Such gowns are of different patterns and types but all are basically adaptations of the Geneva gown of the Reformers.

The use of a gown or robe for pulpit wear has much to commend it. It follows out the tradition of the minister as the teacher (*doctor*) of Christian truth, and as one who is ordained to speak authoritatively regarding it. A gown has also a certain psychological value in setting the minister apart from the people when he is to declare God's word to them. Nor is this apartness something felt by the people alone. What minister worthy of the name has not been aware, as he robed himself to go before a congregation, that he was assuming an awesome but a glorious mission?

194

Last but not least a gown hides with its kind encompassing folds all the vagaries of suiting and discordances of dress that otherwise might be much too evident. "A good gown," one minister put it, "covers a multitude of poor tailoring."

Clerical gowns are all very much alike, though some are designed to hang loosely with no fastening in front, while others fasten closely almost to the neck. The so-called "doctor's gown" is usually worn open and is quite appropriate for both pulpit and academic use. As a rule most ministers wear the gown closed, but some wear it partially open and with it a turndown collar and four-in-hand tie. The minister in such instances must of course be sure that the suit or vest he wears under the gown is black or quite dark so that there will be no incongruity between the black gown and the clothing visible beneath. This caution holds for the necktie also and even for the socks worn. The tie should be black, or black with fine white stripes; the collar wing, poke, or turndown.

A majority of the ministerial authorities who reported on their practice state that they always wear the gown for formal worship, and those who are doctors of divinity wear the doctor's bars—three bars of black velvet on both sleeves. But only a very few favor the use of the academic hood with the gown at regular church services. "The academic hood has no place in church or religious services," Dr. James Gilkey puts it; while a Brooklyn minister termed the use of the hood "vanity and ostentation." It must indeed be admitted that the blazing colors of a man's *alma mater* displayed in broad patterns on his back as he walks into the pulpit do not comport with ordinary Sunday worship. However, if the occasion be an academic one, as at a college commencement, or even the regular formal services at a school or college chapel, the hood is quite in keeping.

The customary pulpit robe ensemble is as follows:

Gown: Always black; worn open or partially open or closed.

Sleeves: May vary, but an inner sleeve that keeps a long expanse of white cuff and shirt from showing when the minister lifts his arm is much to be preferred.

Collar: Any type if the four-in-hand or bow tie is to be visible. A clerical collar if Geneva bands are worn.

Tie: Black bow or black four-in-hand; or black with white stripes permissible as a four-in-hand.

Shoes: Black, as should be the socks.

Hood: For academic occasions; must be fastened carefully.

Shirt: White.

Suit: Any dark suit which if seen below the gown, or through the gown if it is worn open, will not be in too marked a contrast.

Head covering: The traditional "mortar board" cap is all right for academic processions, but when the minister is to wear his gown outdoors for distinctively ministerial service apart from college occasions, a biretta or Cranmer cap would be more appropriate. However, nonliturgical ministers who wear the gown outside the church—which is rare—rebel against the clericalism which such headgear implies. But of course the ordinary hat would be impossible.

Instead of vestments or gown, *formal morning clothes* have for a long time been the clerical wear of many Protestant ministers, and still are in many parts of the country, especially in the South. This costume is based largely upon the cutaway or morning coat, which with gray-and-black striped trousers has long been considered correct formal daytime wear for a gentleman. Formerly the frock coat or "Prince Albert" was frequently seen in place of the cutaway, and is entirely proper. But the frock coat does not find many wearers today among American men, either clerical or lay.

The formal morning costume referred to above has been so

long used by many Protestant nonliturgical ministers that in some sections it has come to be regarded as distinctively clerical attire. The customary ensemble is here indicated:

Coat: Black cutaway, not "cut away" quite as much as that of the ordinary gentleman. No braid; plain uncovered buttons favored by most, though covered buttons are called for by some prominent clergymen. No satin-faced lapels. Cloth is usually some rich, nonshiny material. Black unfinished worsted is much in favor.

Waistcoat or vest: Of the same cloth as the coat. Cut rather high. A silk cassock vest with clerical collar is much favored today with the cutaway by certain clergymen.

Trousers: May be of same cloth as coat; or black-and-gray striped; or black with fine white stripe. Never with cuffs.

Collar: Poke or wing. The turndown collar and four-in-hand, however, is often worn with the cutaway.

Tie: Black bow; or black, or black-and-white four-in-hand.

Shoes: Any good black shoe.

Hat: Should be high silk or opera crush for formal morning clothes, but ministers as well as other men have such a distaste for a "high hat" that a dark Homburg or any distinctive, soft, dark felt is made to do. When an overcoat is worn, this is easier to "get away with." A derby or straw or colored hat of any kind is of course out of the question.

Shirt: Always white. The dress shirt with attached stiff cuffs is correct.

Jewelry: Shirt studs and cuff links to match have always been an institution. These can be of mother-of-pearl or dark onyx, even of gold if inconspicuous. Fashion decrees that if a bow tie is worn with a cutaway, the one shirt stud that shows above the waistcoat must be of gold, though it would not seem that this should be obligatory upon the minister. The four-in-hand, of course, obviates such a situation. Gold cuff links may be worn, or even an inconspicuous scarf pin with a four-in-hand, but the minister who is unadorned with jewelry is in flawless taste.

Gloves: White kid or gray suede or white buck would be most formal, but many use an inconspicuous gray or dark dress glove.

General appearance

A man's clothing and appearance always reflect his personality, and the minister is no exception. While he may feel that he has the right to dress as he pleases, he should not forget that here again he may not divest himself of his essential character in any company; and there is a sense in which a minister is never "off duty." There is a time both for shirt sleeves and for work clothes, but in public or on the street no minister can afford to let his profession down.

Any man, to be well dressed, must be immaculately groomed. His personal appearance must be beyond reproach—hair trimmed, nails clean and well cared for, and clothing at all times clean and pressed. These things are basic of course. Clothes need not be fine, but they do need to be *clean*. A soiled shirt cuff lifted before an audience, or the sight of a dark spot on the shirt where the collar point touches—what an affront to the tremendous "Be ye clean, that bear the vessels of the Lord."

Tan shoes are out for anything like formal wear, especially in the pulpit. Neckties give an opportunity for a bit of color in normal daytime wear, but let there be no colored tie visible in the pulpit. Neither are colored socks proper for pulpit wear. Good taste, of course, keeps any gentleman from wearing an assortment of fobs, pins, chains, buttons, and whatnot on his coat or vest. Whatever jewelry is worn should be simple and inconspicuous.

A schedule of proper ministerial costuming

What has been said above in regard to correct dress may be summed up briefly as follows:

Formal morning worship: One's most formal wear. Vestments, if and as prescribed; pulpit robes with accessories as described; or morning clothes—cutaway, frock coat, or dark single- or double-breasted sack coat with matching trousers, or with dark gray striped trousers as described.

Evening worship: One's formal morning wear not incorrect unless church custom directs otherwise. The cutaway is sometimes worn for evening worship and is not incorrect for ministers, though strictly speaking it is not considered correct evening wear for the ordinary gentleman. The black, dark blue, or dark gray sack suit is often worn by ministers of the nonliturgical churches.

Summer services: Ministers of the nonliturgical churches often dress in light summer clothing on hot Sundays and discard pulpit robes. White linen suits are frequently seen.

Formal weddings: One's formal ecclesiastical dress. If the minister wears a cutaway or regular suit, it is not out of keeping for him to wear a boutonniere if the other gentlemen of the bridal party wear them. If there is to be a reception afterward, it is proper for the minister to attend in his clerical costume; or if he wears a gown for the wedding, he may have evening dress or a Tuxedo on under it and so be ready for the later occasion.

Informal weddings: Depends on circumstances. Even a "quiet home wedding" demands some measure of formality.

Funerals: Always formal ministerial attire, wherever the funeral is held—church, home, or undertaker's. No funeral is ever informal.

Baptism: As baptism is generally held to be one of the sacraments of the Christian Church, the minister should usually be

199

dressed formally for the occasion. In those situations where baptism takes place in a private home circumstances will govern.

Formal secular evening occasions: If the minister has a dinner jacket or full dress, he should feel free to wear it on such occasions just as other men do. If he has not such a garment, or prefers to go in what is his regular clerical garb, he is perfectly correct in so doing.

Sports, fishing expeditions, picnics, etc.: The minister should feel free to wear the same sort of clothes that other men do on such occasions.

It should be added to what has already been said that any formal wear is out of keeping in informal places. When a man's dress makes him unusually conspicuous—as for instance a formal ensemble worn in a rural community where this particular costume has not been customary—although he may be correctly dressed by the standards that prevail in other places, he may lose something by being out of line with the community which he serves. It should be remembered that "usage" comes from "use," and "good usage" is but the crystallization of "usefulness."

Appendix

Below are the five formal codes which are referred to and cited as separate reference items throughout this book. They have never been abrogated or revised in any particular, so far as can be ascertained.

THE CONGREGATIONAL CODE

(Adopted by the New Haven, Connecticut, Association of Congregational Ministers. Quoted in *Church Administration* by William H. Leach, Cokesbury Press, 1931.)

I. *The Minister and His Work*

1. As a minister controls his own time, he should make it a point of honor to give full service to his parish.

2. Part of the minister's service as a leader of his people is to reserve sufficient time for serious study in order thoroughly to apprehend his message, keep abreast of current thought, and develop his intellectual and spiritual capacities.

3. It is equally the minister's duty to keep physically fit. A weekly holiday and an annual vacation should be taken and used for rest and improvement.

4. As a public interpreter of divine revelation and human duty, the minister should tell the truth as he sees it and present it tactfully and constructively.

5. It is unethical for the minister to use sermon material prepared by another without acknowledging the source from which it comes.

6. As an ethical leader in the community, it is incumbent on the minister to be scrupulously honest, avoid debts, and meet his bills promptly.

7. The minister should be careful not to bring reproach on his calling by joining in marriage improper persons.

II. *The Minister's Relations with His Parish*

1. It is unethical for a minister to break his contract made with the church.

2. As a professional man the minister should make his service primary and the remuneration secondary. His efficiency, however, demands that he should receive a salary adequate to the work he is expected to do and commensurate with the scale of living in that parish which he serves.

3. It is unethical for the minister to engage in other lines of remunerative work without the knowledge and consent of the church or its official board.

4. The confidential statements made to a minister by his parishioners are privileged and should never be divulged without the consent of those making them.

5. It is unethical for a minister to take sides with factions in his parish.

6. The minister recognizes himself to be the servant of the community in which he resides. Fees which are offered should be accepted only in the light of this principle.

201

III. *The Minister's Relations with the Profession*

1. It is unethical for a minister to interfere directly or indirectly with the parish work of another minister; especially should he be careful to avoid the charge of proselyting.

2. Ministerial service should not be rendered to the members of another parish without consulting the minister of that parish.

3. It is unethical for a minister to make overtures to or consider overtures from a church whose pastor has not yet resigned.

4. It is unethical for a minister to speak ill of the character or work of another minister, especially of his predecessor or successor. It is the duty of a minister, however, in flagrant cases of unethical conduct, to bring the matter before the proper body.

5. As members of the same profession and brothers in the service of a common Master, the relation between ministers should be one of frankness and cooperation.

THE DISCIPLES CODE

(Adopted by the Committee on Effective Ministry of the Home and State Missions Planning Council of Disciples of Christ. Quoted in *Called—In Honor* by Clarence B. Tupper, Bethany Press.)

MY MINISTERIAL CODE OF ETHICS

I am a minister of the Lord Jesus Christ, called of God to proclaim the unsearchable riches of His love. Therefore, I voluntarily adopt the following principles in order that through dedication and self-discipline I may set a more worthy example for those whom I seek to lead and serve.

I. *My Personal Conduct*

I will cultivate my devotional life, continuing steadfastly in reading the Bible, meditation and prayer.

I will endeavor to keep physically and emotionally fit for my work.

I will be fair to my family and will endeavor to give them the time and consideration to which they are entitled.

I will endeavor to live within my income and will not carelessly leave unpaid debts behind me.

I will strive to grow in my work through comprehensive reading and careful study and by attending conventions and conferences.

I will be honest in my stewardship of money.

I will not plagiarize.

I will seek to be Christlike in my personal attitudes and conduct toward all people regardless of race, class or creed.

II. *My Relationship to the Church Which I Serve*

I will dedicate my time and energy to my Christian ministry and will maintain strict standards of discipline.

In my preaching I will exalt the Bible and will be true to my convictions, proclaiming the same in love.

I will maintain a Christian attitude toward other members of the church staff and will not expect the unreasonable of them.

I will not seek special gratuities.

In my pastoral calling, I will have respect for every home I enter for I am a representative of Christ and the Church.

In my administrative and pastoral duties I will be impartial so no one can truthfully say that I am pastor of only one group in the church.

I will strive with evangelistic zeal to build up my church, but will maintain a Christian attitude at all times toward members of other religious bodies.

I will under no circumstances violate confidences that come to me as a minister.

I will strive to strengthen the congregation when leaving a pastorate regardless of the circumstances.

III. *My Relationship to Fellow Ministers*

I will refuse to enter into unfair competition with other ministers in order to secure a pulpit or place of honor.

I will seek to serve my fellow ministers and their families in every way possible and in no instance will I accept fees for such services.

I will refrain from speaking disparagingly about the work of either my predecessor or my successor.

I will refrain from frequent visits to a former field and if, in exceptional cases, I am called back for a funeral or a wedding, I will request that the resident minister be invited to participate in the service.

I will never embarrass my successor by meddling in the affairs of the church I formerly served.

I will be courteous to any predecessor of mine when he returns to the field, and will be thoughtful of any retired minister.

I will, upon my retirement from the active ministry, give my pastor loyal support.

I will not gossip about other ministers.

I will hold in sincere respect any minister whose work is well done, regardless of the size or the nature of the field he serves.

I will consider all ministers my co-laborers in the work of Christ and even though I may differ from them I shall respect their Christian earnestness and sincerity.

IV. *My Relationship to the Community*

I will strive to be human in all my relationships to the community but will never lower my ideals in order to appear "a good fellow."

I will not be a party to funeral or marriage rackets.

I will be considerate of the working hours of business and professional men and will not consume their time with unimportant matters.

MINISTERIAL ETHICS AND ETIQUETTE

I consider that my first duty to my community is to be a conscientious pastor and leader of my own congregation, but I will not use this fact as an easy excuse to escape reasonable responsibilities that the community calls upon me to assume.

V. *My Relationship to My Communion*

I will at all times recognize that I am a part of a fellowship that has made large contributions to my church, my education, and my ministry. In view of this fact I acknowledge a debt of loyalty to my communion and will strive to fulfill my obligations by co-operating in its efforts to extend the Kingdom of God.

VI. *My Relationship to the Church Universal*

I will give attention, sympathy and, when possible, support to the Ecumenical Church, recognizing that my church is a part of the Church Universal.

METHODIST MINISTERS' ETHICAL CODE

(Adopted by a group of Methodist ministers meeting in conference at Rockford, Illinois. Quoted in the *Christian Century*, December 16, 1926.)

When a Methodist minister becomes a member of the conference he promises to employ all of his time in the work of God. We again call attention to the fact that he is thus honor bound to give full service to his parish.

Part of the minister's service as a leader of his people is to reserve sufficient time for serious study in order thoroughly to appreciate his message, keep abreast of current thought, and develop his intellectual and spiritual capacities.

It is equally the minister's duty to keep physically fit. A weekly holiday and an annual vacation should be taken and used for rest and improvement.

As a public interpreter of divine revelation and human duty, the minister should tell the truth as he sees it and present it tactfully and constructively.

It is unethical for the minister to use sermon material prepared by another without acknowledging the source from which it comes.

As an ethical leader in the community, it is incumbent on the minister to be scrupulously honest, avoid debts, and meet his bills promptly.

The minister should be careful not to bring reproach upon his calling by joining in marriage improper persons.

As a professional man the minister should make his service primary and the remuneration secondary. This implies a salary, paid regularly, and adequate to the work he is expected to do and commensurate with the scale of living in that parish where he serves.

The confidential statements made to a minister by his parishioners are privileged and should never be divulged without the consent of those making them.

In the making of conference reports, it is unethical for a minister to report other than the actual salary received.

The minister recognizes himself to be the servant of the community in which he resides. Fees which are offered should be accepted only in the light of this principle.

It is unethical for a minister to interfere directly or indirectly with the parish work of another minister; especially should he be careful to avoid the charge of proselyting.

Ministerial service should not be rendered to the members of another parish without consulting the minister of the parish, or by invitation from him.

It is unethical for a minister to speak ill of the character or work of another minister, especially of his predecessor or successor. It is the duty of a minister, however, in flagrant cases of unethical conduct, to bring the matter before the proper body.

It is unethical for a minister on leaving a charge to leave the parsonage property in other than in first-class condition, with all dirt, rubbish, etc., removed. Common courtesy to his successor demands the observance of the golden rule.

As members of the same profession and brothers in the service of a common Master, the relation between ministers should be one of frankness, of comradeship, and of co-operation.

THE PRESBYTERIAN CODE

(Reported as adopted by the New York Presbytery. Quoted in an article by William H. Leach in *The Methodist Quarterly Review*, July, 1927.)

I. *Personal Standards*

1. As a minister controls his own time, he should make it a point of honor to give full service to his parish.

2. Part of a minister's service as a leader of his people is to reserve sufficient time for serious study in order to thoroughly apprehend his message, keep abreast of current thought, and develop his intellectual and spiritual capacities.

3. It is equally the minister's duty to keep physically fit. A weekly holiday and an annual vacation should be taken and used for rest and improvement.

4. It is unethical for a minister to use sermon material prepared by another, without acknowledging the source from which it comes.

5. As an ethical leader in the community, it is incumbent on the minister to be scrupulously honest, avoid debts, and meet his bills promptly.

II. *Relations with the Parish*

1. In accepting a pastorate, a minister assumes obligations which he should faithfully perform until released in the constitutional manner.

2. As a professional man, the minister should make his service primary and the remuneration secondary.

3. A minister should not regularly engage in other kinds of remunerative work, except with the knowledge and consent of the official board of the Church.

4. The confidential statements made to a minister by his parishioners are sacred and not to be divulged.

5. As a minister is especially charged to study the peace and unity of the Church, it is unwise as well as unethical for a minister to take sides with any faction in his Church, in any but exceptional cases.

6. The minister is the servant of the community and not only of his Church, and should find in the opportunity for general ministerial service a means of evidencing the Christian spirit.

III. Relations with the Profession

1. It is unethical for a minister to interfere directly or indirectly with the parish work of another minister; especially should he be careful to avoid the charge of proselyting from a sister Church.

2. Except in emergencies, ministerial service should not be rendered to the members of another parish without the knowledge of the minister of the parish.

3. A minister should not make overtures to or consider overtures from a Church whose pastor has not yet resigned.

4. It is unethical for a minister to speak ill of the character or work of another minister, especially of his predecessor or successor. It is the duty of a minister, however, in cases of flagrant misconduct to bring the matter before the proper body.

5. A minister should be very careful to protect his brother ministers from imposition by unworthy applicants for aid, and should refer such cases to established charitable agencies rather than to send them to other Churches.

6. A minister should be scrupulously careful in giving indorsements to agencies or individuals unless he has a thorough knowledge and approval of their work lest such indorsements be used to influence others unduly.

7. As members of the same profession and brothers in the service of a common Master, the relation between ministers should be one of frankness and co-operation.

UNITARIAN MINISTERS' CODE OF ETHICS

(Adopted by the Unitarian Ministerial Union. Quoted in *Church Management*, August, 1926.)

I. The Minister and His Task

1. The minister should always place service above profit, avoiding the suspicion of an inordinate love of money, and never measuring his work by his salary.

2. He should be conscientious in giving full time and strength to the work of his church, engaging in avocations and other occupations in such a way and to such a degree as not to infringe unduly upon that work unless some definite arrangement for part-time service is made with his church.

3. The minister should count it a most important part of his work to keep in touch with the best religious thought of his day, and should make it a point of honor to set aside sufficient time for reading and study.

4. It is the minister's duty to keep himself in as good physical condition as possible.

5. The minister should set a high moral standard of speech and conduct. He should be scrupulous in the prompt payment of bills, and careful in the incurring of financial obligations.

6. The minister should never speak disparagingly of his church or his profession.

II. *The Minister and His Church Officials*

1. The minister's relation to his parish is a sacred contract, which should not be terminated by him, or broken by his resignation, without at least three months' notice, except by special agreement.

2. The minister is the recognized leader of the parish, but he should not assume authority in church affairs which is not expressly granted to him by the terms of his contract, or the usage of his office, or the vote of his church.

3. The minister rightfully controls his own pulpit, but he should not invite persons into it who are not generally acceptable to the parish, and he should be ready to accede to all reasonable requests by responsible church officials for its use.

III. *The Minister and His Parishioners*

1. The minister should remember that he is pastor of all his people. He should avoid the display of preferences, and the cultivation of intimacies within the parish which may be construed as evidence of partiality. He should not attach himself to any social set either in the church or in the community. He should not allow personal feelings to interfere with the impartial nature of his ministrations.

2. In the case of parish controversy, the minister should maintain an attitude of good will to all, even when he himself is the subject of controversy.

3. It is unethical to divulge the confidences of parishioners without their consent.

4. Professional service should be gladly rendered to all, without regard to compensation, except for necessary expenses incurred.

IV. *The Minister and His Brother Ministers*

1. It is unethical for a minister to render professional service within the parish of another minister, or to occupy another minister's pulpit, without the consent of that minister, whenever obtainable, and this consent should be given readily.

2. He should be very careful not to proselytize among the members of another church.

3. He should discourage all overtures from a church whose minister has not yet resigned.

4. He should always speak with good will of another minister, especially of the minister who has preceded or followed him in a parish. It may be his duty, however, to bring to the attention of the responsible officials of the

fellowship any instance of gross professional or personal misconduct that may injure the good name of the ministry.

5. The minister should be very generous in responding to reasonable requests for assistance from his brother ministers and his denominational officials, remembering that he is one of a larger fellowship.

6. It is his duty to show a friendly and co-operative interest in his brethren, attending the group meetings of the ministers, assisting his brother ministers with labors of love, defending them against injustice, and following them with kindly concern in their hours of need or distress.

7. He should never accept from a brother minister fees for professional services at christenings, weddings, and funerals.

V. *The Minister and His Community*

1. The minister is not under obligations to marry every couple that comes to him to be married. The power of refusal, however, should be exercised with great discretion.

2. The minister's responsibility to the state is that of a citizen. He should, therefore, be faithful to his public obligations, and should respond to reasonable requests for assistance in community work.

INDEX